I mean that literally, because in my research for this and my other retail books, I researched the best retail stores across the globe.

Most retailers underestimate the relevance of store design and visual merchandise display to their success.

Your selling environment determines the customers you attract and the price you can charge.

The retail business is 'showbiz.' The extent to which you are willing to put up a great performance for your customers is the extent to which you are going to succeed.

The goal of this book is to teach you the psychology and strategies behind a beautiful visual merchandise display.

Harrods success is based upon three things:

- Good store design
- Beautiful visual merchandise display
- Effective loss prevention strategies

My aim is to teach you how to replicate a Harrods-like visual merchandise display to enable you to sell a made in China toy bus for three times the price it is sold for by other retailers.

This book is not about changing or improving upon what you are already doing; it is about the hidden opportunities in your retail business you have not paid attention to.

It is my guarantee to you that you will easily triple or even quadruple your profit margin in less than 90 days by implementing a third of the information in this book.

During my research for this book, I visited Harrods. I have heard a lot about Harrods, but had not actually visited it. When my sister visited me from the States, Harrods was on her list of places to visit. However, by the time we arrived it was already closed for the day.

You can imagine my anticipation and apprehension at visiting one of the most famous retail stores where royalties, Hollywood A-list stars and the "who is who" from around the world go shopping.

In my mind, everything in Harrods was made of gold. I even bought a special outfit for the occasion to ensure I was in sync with the royalties and A-list stars.

I was hoping I could catch a glimpse of Roman Abramovich and some of his billionaire friends or some Saudi prince.

However, instead of Russian oligarch or Middle East Sheikh, what caught my attention was a bus.

I had bought the identical bus for my son from ASDA. It was the same bus in the same packaging.

An odd question popped into my mind when I noticed the bus: why is it that the same bus, in the same packaging, probably made in the same factory in China, by the same people, being sold in Harrods for almost three times the price it was sold for in ASDA?

At first it was a mystery to me. But as I walked around Harrods the answer came to me.

ASDA sells toy bus. Harrods sells classy toy bus even if it is made in the same factory in China.

There is a distinction and that distinction is what this book is about.

The price of a product is not determined by the cost of bringing that product to the marketplace as we are taught in business school, rather by *who is buying, how much they are willing to pay and how the product is sold.*

The reason the same bus, made in the same factory in Chine is sold in Harrods almost three times the price it is sold for in ASDA comes down to *who shops at Harrods and how the bus is sold to them.*

For a start, cheapskates like me are not Harrods target market. Harrods know their target market is oil Sheikhs and Russian oligarchs whose focus is not on the products but on the manner in which the product is sold to them.

This is a very important point I will like you to take from this book. Most retailers fail because they ignore this simple but fundamental marketing principle. The majority of retailers do not even know their target market.

They open their stores, stock them with goods and hope that customers will show up simply because they are open for business.

This is a very big mistake!

You first need to decide who you want to sell to and then create a selling environment to attract those types of people.

Harrods have obviously decided who they want to sell to, therefore, they created a selling environment that appeals to only those types of people.

Their store design and visual merchandise display are created to appeal to their target customers.

Harrods has one of the best store design and visual merchandise display in the retail industry…Period.

About the Author

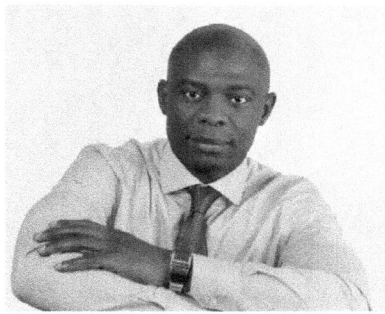

Romeo Richards is the founder of the Business Education Centre, an institute that shows professional entrepreneurs such as doctors, lawyers, dentists, consultants, trainers, coaches, and security firm owners how to make "7 Figure" in twelve months. He is also the creator of the Business Success Quadrangle Framework and The Blue Ocean Strategy Canvas for: doctors, lawyers, dentists, consultants, retailers, coaches, trainers and security firms.

He has authored eight books on retail profit improvement and is currently writing four additional books on retail store design, visual merchandising, how to market a retail store and how to make profit in retail and the "How to effectively market and manage a professional firm" series for doctors, lawyers, dentists, consultants, trainers, coaches and security firms.

He has authored several White Papers and regularly writes articles on entrepreneur development, retail profit improvement and speak on the same.

Visual Merchandise

How to Create a Beautiful yet Profitable Display

Romeo Richards

www.theprofitexperts.co.uk

+44(0)78 650 49508

romeo@theprofitexperts.co.uk

© Copyright Protected; 2013. The Business Education Center. All Rights Reserved.

Dedication

I wrote about vision as your reason for doing anything. I do what I do first and foremost to be an example to my son.

Secondly, to have the ability to help my people shed the curse of poverty.

Alex this book is for you!

Africa this book is in your honour!

Table of Contents

About the Book i

About the Author v

Dedication ix

Acknowledgements xiii

Why You Should Read This Book xvii

Introduction xix

Chapter One: The Psychology Of Visual Merchandising Display 1

Chapter Two: How To Use Visual Merchandising To Increase Sales 13

Chapter Three: Challenges Facing Visual Merchandisers 29

Chapter Four: How To Burst The Price Myth With Creative Merchandise Display 41

Chapter Five: The Best Merchandise Display Strategy 57

Chapter Six: How To Maximise Display Space Allocation With Creative Display 71

Chapter Seven: The Benefits Planogram Software 83

Chapter Eight: How To Profitably Display Merchandise 97

Summary 107

Great Books by Romeo 109

Book Romeo 118

Acknowledgements

My sincere gratitude to Mr. White, John and Michael for editing the book.

Thanks Jen for formatting it and Joseph for managing the entire project.

Visual Merchandise

How to Create a Beautiful yet Profitable Display

Romeo Richards

www.theprofitexperts.co.uk

+44(0)78 650 49508

romeo@theprofitexperts.co.uk

Why You Should Read This Book

Why should you read this book when there are literally thousands of visual merchandise display books on the market?

For a start, it is the only book on visual merchandise display that talks about the only thing you are interested in: Profit.

How can you make profit in your retail store?

You make profit by:

- Increasing sales
- Increasing customer satisfaction
- Increasing staff productivity
- Decreasing shrinkage

In this book, we teach you how to achieve the above objectives through the use of beautiful yet secure visual merchandise display.

No other book on visual merchandise display has ever connected visual merchandise display to those four critical success factors and profit.

There are fundamental principles which underpin good visual merchandise display:

- Customer attraction
- Persuasion to buy
- Shrinkage management

Your ability to effectively embed these elements into your visual merchandise display strategy will determine your level of success. This book outlines the process for embedding those three elements into your visual merchandise display and sales strategy.

It outlines the best visual merchandise display strategies used by the most successful retailers in the world...Strategies, when effectively applied will propel you to unbelievable success.

And here is the icing on the cake; your competitors do not even know most of these strategies. So what you have in your hand is the missing piece of the retail success secret...The ultimate visual merchandise display blueprint secret.

Introduction – Visual Merchandise Display

If you are a horror film Junkie you always know when a horror film is about to reach its climax.

If the scene is set in a house, you will notice the camera moving up and down the stairs…then the window flings open…and the moon starts shinning directly into the room…wind begins to blow…the light starts blinking on and off…on and off…and you hear the clock tick…tick…tick…then there is the sound of footsteps in the corridor…then the shadow of the antagonist appears…and then zoom!…without warning the antagonist attacks.

In horror film after horror film, this identical scene plays out all the time. Whether the film is being shot in a house, in the night or day or out in the woods, the costume design and the choreography is always the same.

Why is this always the case with horror and the more successful films?

Answer: The directors of horror films understand that the intrigue of the film is not just about the killing or the plot. It is also about the costume design, the sound, the lights, and the background.

When someone goes to watch a horror film, they already know someone is going to die. Therefore the directors understand that the killings no longer scare the audience, it is the events leading to the killing that are intriguing.

What does horror film have to do with visual merchandise display and what lesson can the retail industry learn from horror films?

The lesson the retail industry can learn from horror films is this: It is not about the merchandise; it is the presentation of the merchandise that matters to the customer.

A good visual merchandise display captures the imagination of its targeted audiences just like a good film does. The store is a theatre where customers come to watch spectacular displays of merchandises. If they like the display they will buy; if they don't like the display, they will leave.

The success of great films stems from their ability to cleverly manipulate people's psychology through the brilliant use of words and costume design.

Retailers can do well to emulate the cleverness of the film industry in the presentation of their merchandise if they intent on achieving similar success.

This books aims to show retailers how to choreograph their visual merchandise display process to achieve similar success.

The first half of the book deals with the psychology of visual merchandise display. It addresses questions for understanding your target market and the various strategies for thinking through your visual merchandise display strategy.

Part two deals with the implementation of visual merchandise display. It outlines the best strategies for implementing an effective visual merchandise display strategy.

Your success as a retailer rests on your ability to create the type of shopping environment that will entice shoppers to visit your store.

The retail environment is changing. These days you are not only competing against other retailers, you are also up against some guy sat in his room selling stuff on the internet.

Consequently, you need to understand that the strategies that worked a few years ago will not work in the new retail environment.

You need a new strategy.

This book contains the new strategies you need to succeed.

Chapter One

The Psychology Of Visual Merchandising Display

Visual merchandising is basically a truncation for marketing in retail. Selling takes place when customers and shoppers show interest in a product and the intention to buy a product on display.

However, before arriving at that conclusion; the individual needs to be sold which is why merchandising is very critical for a retail store. Most people do not buy because they are uninterested in a product or service been sold to them. And it is very difficult to sell to an unmotivated person.

So how do you motivate a person?

You do that by selling them what they want.

This brings us to the next question.

What does everyone want?

In marketing we are taught to believe that everyone wants a different thing.

This statement is true to an extent but it's not quite true. Human psychology has not changed since the dawn of time. The same desires we harboured when we lived in caves, we still hold dear today.

Every shopper, client or customer wants basically the following three things:

- ➢ Result

➤ Solution

➤ Relief from something

These three things manifest themselves in the form of the products and services we choose to buy. However, in the final analysis when someone takes out his credit card to buy a product or service no matter what that product or service is, they are doing so to satisfy all or at least one of the above.

Being aware of that, as you prepare to display your merchandise, the questions that need to be going through your mind are the following:

- Which one of the above three are you marketing to satisfy in a particular display?
- When someone passes your shop window, and they take a glimpse of your display, what emotion are you aiming to trigger?
- What result should they imagine the display is going to produce for them?
- What solution should they think your display would provide?
- Finally what pain is the display going to relieve?

This is classic marketing 101.

Your merchandise does not necessarily have to produce those results for the shopper; it just needs to produce the perception of the result in the shoppers' mind.

But there is a catch: the person creating the display needs to know the benefit behind the benefit (the solution the shopper is seeking).

It is only when your visual merchandiser know the benefit behind the benefit will they be able to create a beautiful attractive display that captivates their targeted audience.

I will use La Senza as an example. A woman passing by a La Senza store, spots a sexy lingerie on display in the window; her first thought is: I will look sexy in that underwear or that bra looks to be just right for me.

Figure 1: Think of the benefit behind the benefit in your display

But here is the interesting part, she would like the bra to prop up her cleavage not because she just wants them cleavage propped up. She wants her cleavage propped up to attract the attention of the opposite sex. (I must add a disclaimer that here that I am not trying to be sexist; I am just using this as an example).

Therefore as a visual merchandiser your aim in creating a display for that lady should not be about the cleavage, but the opposite sex. Your goal needs to be to match the thinking process that lady in your display.

Do not create a display to appeal to the beauty of her breast but the impression that the beautiful breast will have – on the opposite sex!

You see that with travel agencies. When you enter a travel agency, what do you see?

The images of a beautiful beach, with a couple or an individual sun bathing and a stunning hotel in the background.

No mention of the eight hours flight to get there, not to mention the two hours check in time at the airport, screaming kids on the airplane, the rude cabin crew and lest I forget...the sleeping air controller.

There is never any mention of those. All they paint for you is the picture of perfect get away that you cannot wait to buy.

As a visual merchandiser, this is the type of picture you want to paint with your display. A major part of visual merchandising is being able to analyse people's thought process.

The human thought process is complex and irrational. Even though he tries to rationalise his actions with artificial explanations of his environment, the reality this: we all do things for the same three reasons:

- Status
- Survival
- Sex

I am aware this might sound like a little over simplistic explanation of the complexity of the human thought process. However, the more you understand your target market, the more you will come to the conclusion that indeed all human actions can be reduced to the three.

As a visual merchandiser your ability to capture these three in your presentation is the key to your success.

The human has three brains:

- Reptile
- Mammal

> Thinker

The problem we face as humans, those three brains are not integrated. They all work separately and the thinking part of the brain is the least dominant of three, which why our thinking process is in most cases, irrational.

In his ground breaking book: "Blink", author Malcolm Glawell brilliantly illustrates this point when he introduces the concept of "the power of thin slicing" and "rapid cognition" which is the type of thinking process that occurs in a blink of an eye.

Thin-slicing is a psychological term for the ability to find patterns in events based upon minimal information. It means making rapid decisions with the least amount of information.

When someone walks through a shopping mall of three hundred stores or on a busy High Street on Saturday afternoon, his mind races and he thinks at a fast rate.

The decision as to which store he enters is made in the blink of an eye. It depends on the merchandise display that catches his attention. Except of course if he had pre-planned a visit to a particular store; he is thin slicing each store as he walks along.

Many of our actions, behaviour and thinking originate from the adaptive unconscious which the majority of us are unaware of. Almost all the time, our decisions are based upon triggers from the unconscious.

> *The good news is that other humans are capable of altering these unconscious biases just by tinkering with miniature details.*

Malcolm Glawell spoke about the tinkering or social engineering process in his first book "The Tipping Point". In "The Tipping Point" he outlines minute details of product packaging for example, that causes a product to tip (increase sales).

The retail landscape is changing rapidly. Endless choices, interruptions and information from all directions are either confusing customers or overwhelming them.

As the shopper walks through the shopping mall, there are a gazillion things going through his mind. Yours is not the only display in the shopping mall neither is it not the only display he has seen on that day.

There are clusters of information and displays all around them. Therefore your job as a visual merchandiser is to ensure that yours stand tall above the rest. That can only be done when you understand the psychology and design your display to suit customers' desire.

People don't like to be sold but they love to buy, therefore your visual presentation should sell to them without appearing to sell to them.

The most effective visual merchandise displays are those that speak directly to a customer's desire for:

- Result
- Solution
- Relief from something

Remember! It is all about:

Status

Survival

Sex

How to implement the psychology of a visual merchandise display

Starbucks has become the favourite hangout for many professionals. But if you went into a Starbucks you will notice that there is nothing special about it. It does not have special decoration or a seat that makes it stand out from all other cafés yet that's exactly what it does…standout above the rest of the cafés.

Apple retail stores are simple, there is nothing sophisticated and stylish about them yet they standout stores in any mall. Apple stores are fast becoming a favourite hangout for shoppers.

So what is it about Starbucks or Apple that makes them stand out?

Answer: Simplicity and elegance!

The fundamental principle that underpins an effective presentation is clarity of message and enhancement. Every presentation carries a message. It can be explicit or implicit; so long as it speaks to a targeted audience.

It is very important that your audience gets the message that your presentation is sending to them.

When the London 2012 logo was unveiled the head of the London 2012 organising committee went through pains of explaining what the logo depicted to the British public.

Figure 2: London 2012 Olympic logo confused everyone

Except for him and probably the designers of the logo, no one else in the UK seemed to have understood the logo. As far as most Brits were concerned, it might have been Greek or symbols from some Hindu alphabet.

When people were interviewed about what they made of the logo, some people described it as children drawing from a nursery…

For some it was an angry person expressing their feelings.

Not a single person associated it with the Olympics. That is a classic example of a presentation gone wrong.

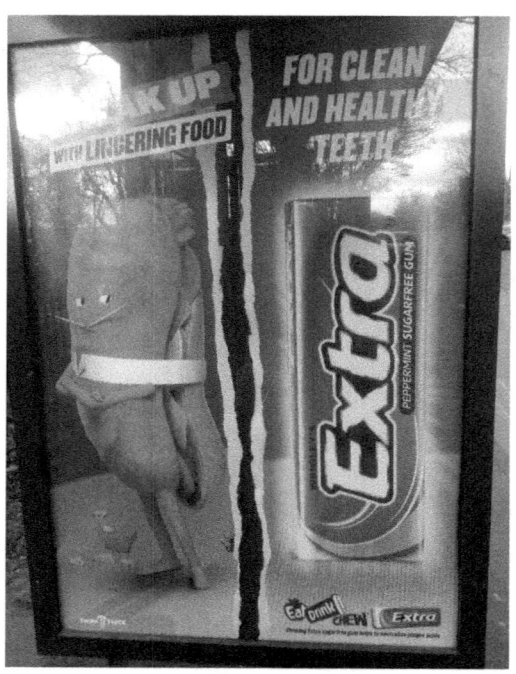

Figure 3: what is the connection between bread and chewing gum?

This is the image of an ad I noticed at the bus stop on my way to the post office. It is an ad for a chewing gum. But as you can see it has the image of a big loaf of bread and the chewing gum on the side.

What exactly is the relation between a chewing gum and a loaf of bread?

As I walked around I constantly see ads on billboards and street corners that do not speak to any specific target audience.

Walking around the shopping mall and in retail store I cannot help but notice several visual merchandise displays even in large retailers that speak to no one in particular.

When creating a visual merchandise display you need to adhere to the following guidelines:

- The display has to be unambiguous so that it can be instantly understood by the targeted audience
- The display must invoke confidence in the brand
- The most important element of the display has to be the biggest and dominant feature of the display

Every single component of the display must be a part of the message you are trying to convey. There can be no component of the display that is there simply to make the display beautiful and more attractive; it must be a part of the overall message.

Colours have to be used sparingly. Colours have to complement one another and be in sync with the rest of the products in the store.

Visual Merchandise Psychology Process

Step One
Know thy customers – Identify your target market.

Step Two
Find out what result, solution and relief they are aiming to achieve with your product.

Step Three

Find the benefit behind the benefit they are trying to achieve (the guy with the muscular body for which they need that bra to prop up their cleavage).

Step Four

Create a visual display that speaks directly to their needs.

How to identify your target market

This is marketing 101 which every business should already know, therefore I am not going dig deep into it.

However, small retailers who might not have the luxury of hiring an expert visual merchandiser might find the following steps helpful:

Step One

After creating the display, speak to staff members and ask them to describe the display for you in their own words. If they explain it in words that you expect your customers to use then you know you have nailed it. This needs to be done every single time you tinker with the display.

Step Two

Speak to your customers – ask them what they think about the display. Ask them what message the display sends to them. If your customers describe your display using words that indicate that they got it, you know you have achieved your objectives.

Step Three

Ask your customers why they buy certain things from your store. When you know why they buy, you will know the result they are trying to achieve with your products.

Step Four

To be able to ascertain the benefit behind the benefit, find out what they intend to do with your products after they have bought it.

For example if a lady came to your store to buy lingerie. By asking her a few probing but un-intrusive questions as she tries them on, you will know if she is single and going out on a date or she is dressing for her spouse.

The more similar answers you receive the easier it would be to present your display to suite them.

Finally ensure your display does not look like the London 2012 logo. It should not confuse your audience; it needs to speak directly to their needs. When they look at it…blink they need to see the result, solution and relief they seek.

Chapter Two

How To Use Visual Merchandising To Increase Sales

Retail success depends on the image you create in your customer's mind about your merchandise as well as your provision of good customer services. Good visual merchandising also helps to create a positive customer image about your store and your products.

All of that results in increases sales.

But retailers tend to overlook the role visual merchandising plays in increasing sales.

Within the last few decades, the retail industry has recognised the role of visual merchandising display in increasing sales.

This is especially true for supermarkets that have mastered the art of visual merchandising display to the point of excellence.

Visual Merchandising display in a retail store:

- Enables consumers to easily locate products
- Keeps customers updated on the latest trends
- Influences customer buying decision
- Creates a pleasant shopping experience

Visual Merchandising display is basically what the shoppers sees either when passing by a retail store or when they are inside the store. It creates a positive image of the store which results in attention, interest, desire and action on the part of the customer.

Simply defined visual merchandising display is the art and science of displaying products to influence shoppers buying decision.

The most aggressive application of visual merchandise displays is used by larger retailers. For instance, sport brands such as Reebok spend 25% of their advertising on point of sale merchandising.

Furthermore, there has been a significant increase in impulse buying of certain products: that is directly attributed ingenuous visual merchandising display.

How to use visual merchandise to increase sales

Known in retail as the "silent salesperson", a good visual merchandising display:

- Presents the product to shoppers
- Invites the shoppers to get closer to the product
- Encourages shoppers to make a purchase
- Tells shoppers everything they need to know about products without the need to make inquiries

Visual Merchandising is a proven formula for increasing retail sales and customer satisfaction. It makes it easier for customers to see products on display as they walk around the store and aids in locating products easily.

The following are the three display structure used in retail stores. A retailer may choose to use the three structures in depending on his product range or he could use any of the three depending on his target market:

- Store-Front
- Window Display
- Found-Space Display

The most important element of visual merchandising display is the shop window display. The shop window display attracts shoppers as they walk pass and entice them to enter the store. There are lots of people who might have no intention of shopping on a particular day. However, the attractiveness of your window display could entice them into your store.

Display windows are usually facing the shopping mall or main shopping street and are geared towards attracting passers-by and enticing them to enter a retail store.

The storefront display is designed to build your brand image and tell the right story of your organisation. When developing the concept for your storefront, create the design from the customer's prospective.

VISUAL MERCHANDISE: HOW TO CREATE A BEAUTIFUL YET PROFITABLE DISPLAY

Figure 4: The storefront display is designed to build your brand image and tell the right story of your organisation

You basically need to enter the customer's mind and ask yourself the question:

> What would my customers see when they look at my storefront display?
> What would they feel as they pass by my storefront?

The answers to those questions should inform your display design and structure.

When planning a window display take into consideration the following:

- The building façade
- The street
- Your target market and their perceptions
- Color harmony
- Lighting
- Viewing angles

Window displays are more successful when a central theme is carried throughout the display; whether the featured products are fashion-oriented, institutional or promotional in nature.

Window displays need to be constantly updated, preferably on a weekly basis or as often as possible. This sends a message to customers that there is always something new going on in the store.

Showcase Display

Figure 5: Showcase Displays feature expensive merchandises

Showcase Displays feature expensive merchandises retailers do not want to be seen in the front store window. They are usually exclusive items that require high security measures. These displays are usually located in high traffic areas in the store to ensure maximum customer attention. The lesser the items in the display, the more the perceived value, resulting in higher priced.

Found-Space Display

Figure 6: Found-Space Displays are displays of products at less prominent areas of the store

Found-Space Displays are displays of products at less prominent areas of the store, such as the top of shelves. When done right, they support your brand image and reiterate the story you want to tell with the display.

Below are points to consider when creating store displays for increased sales:

Install signage

Figure 7: Store signage needs to be appropriately installed

Store signage needs to be appropriately installed and placed in a position that allows shoppers to read the information written on them from across the aisle. A sign is a silent salesperson and a huge part of the shopper's first impression of your store.

Like Apple simplicity, clarity, elegance and legibility need to be the rule of thumb.

Use the appropriate colour

Figure 8: Your colour usage will significantly contribute to shopper's impression of your store

Your colour usage will significantly contribute to shopper's impression of your store as they pass by it. The store colour needs to be suitably chosen as it can influence your customer's mood.

The wall colours need to correspond with the carpet, floor tiles or the fixtures.

Lighting system

Figure 9: Lighting increases the visibility of the merchandise

The store should be appropriately lit and well ventilated. Lighting increases the visibility of the merchandise. A properly lit store contributes to the promotion of specific products and the store's image.

Store window lights should be strong enough to overcome the reflections from outside.

Contextual Product Display

Figure 10: Group together products in their respective racks

Group together products in their respective racks and place associated labels on the same shelves. This helps your customers locate products easily. The merchandise should be appropriately and neatly placed and should not fall off the shelves.

The latest trend items should be cleverly displayed on the shelves to attract customers and entice them to buy. Expensive and unique products should be placed on the right side of the store as most people are right handed and tend to gravitate towards the right side of the store.

Old merchandise should be removed as quickly as practically possible and placed on sale to create an atmosphere of constant freshness in the store.

Identify the right furniture and fixtures

Figure 11: All unnecessary furniture should be removed

All unnecessary furniture should be removed to create enough space for customers to move freely in the store. The more comfortable your store, the higher your chances of retaining customers, which will result in increased sales.

Maintaining an area for spouses or children to read or play and for physically challenged kids or elderly customers to rest also contributes to a good customer experience.

Providing resting space is a difficult concept to sell to store planners because of the cost of retail space. However, the payoff far outweighs the cost as the longer shoppers stay in your store, the higher the chances of them buying.

A changing room is an important component of a clothing store as it increases the possibility of the customer buying if they have had the chance of trying the cloth and it fits them well.

Separate changing rooms for male and female or a comfortable non-gender specific open space with individual cubicles will suffice.

Maintain good ambiance

Figure 12: The store ambience is essential for attracting new customers and retaining existing ones

Playing music that appeals to your target market can have a positive effect on your customers. Loud music is not advisable as it hinders effective communication between the customer and store associates.

Playing music that appeals to your target market is another strategy for keeping customers longer in your store.

The store ambience is also essential for attracting new customers and retaining existing ones. Customers shy away from untidy stores; therefore, ensure your store is tidy at all times.

The friendlier and more relaxing you can make your store, the longer your customers will stay and eventually make purchase.

Sometimes the store's appearance is more important than products in terms of a customer's decision to enter your store. Ensure your store entrance is welcoming; that your visual merchandise display tells the story of your store and merchandise display is resulting in higher sales.

How to implement a good visual merchandise display that increases sales

The following are the basic steps for creating visual merchandise display that increases sales:

Step One
Select a theme that tells the story

There needs to always be a theme or story that is being communicated to your potential customers in your display. Develop a theme around the reason why you decide to display some specific product in the window.

- Who are the characters in your display?
- Where are they going and why?
- How old are they?
- What jobs do they do?
- What merchandise would help you tell your product story better?
- If the story is about living a healthy lifestyle, what could you integrate into your theme to help you silently make this point in the display?
- If your story is about Christmas, Valentine or outdoor adventure, what are the details that will make your story come alive?

You can take your story to a whole new level with the use of props and mannequins. Just as if you were writing a story, your display needs to answer these questions:

- How old are your target market?
- What do they do?
- Where are they going?
- What season is it?

You can also provide each mannequin a name to bring them to life. The key is to clearly understand who you are creating the display for and what message you want to convey to them through the display.

Step Two
Know thy customer

One of the major reasons for the failure of most retail ventures is that most retailers do not know their target market. This is marketing 101: It is critical for your success as a business. If you do not know who you serve, you might not be serving anyone.

> Who are your costumers?
> Are they teenagers, young professionals, college students or young couples?
> Are they housewives?
> Are they Single mums?
> Are they women in their 40's with lots of discretionary income?
> Do your customers want a bargain or are they looking for something unique?
> What interests them?

Answering the above questions will ensure that the message of your display is clearly understood by your target market. If your display does not target a particular segment of your market, it will not sell.

Step Three
Identify your Competitors

It is critical that you know who your competitors are; their product offering and service provision. By having an understanding of the strength and weaknesses of your competition, you can better prepare a display that either directly rivals or is better than theirs.

Competitive analysis is the key to the success of any business. Knowing the strength and weaknesses of your competition is a key element in your success as a retailer.

Step Four
Choose the right products for your store window
Your storefront is a window to your store. The products displayed their, provide potential customers an idea of the products inside the store. Consequently, it is imperative that you choose the products that are displayed in the shop window carefully.

You need to display products that are the most representative of products in your store.

Ensure that products that are displayed in the storefront are available in the store. It does not speak well of your store if shoppers are attracted to the store because of products they see in the storefront display but when they enter the store to buy that product, it is unavailable. Remember that the unavailability of product can result in a frustrated and unhappy customer.

Do not overcrowd the storefront with too much merchandise. The message you are trying to send to potential customers could be lost in an overcrowded window. Window displays should be in complete harmony with the entire atmosphere of the store.

Step Five
Observe the effect of display on your customers
An effective way to attract customers is to have good exterior and interior displays. As customers pass by your display, you need to have a procedure for measuring the effect of your display on them.

  Does your display window inspire your customers?
  Is it pleasing to the eye and does it have a welcoming effect?

Ensure you display your merchandise as it would be used in a real life scenario and that it is kept simple but striking to have a great impact.

Ensure that your window display can be seen from a distance to draw your potential customers inside your store. You might have the most creative idea, however, if you are incapable of displaying it in such a way that it grabs your shoppers attention as they pass by your store, you have defeated the purpose of the display.

The key to increasing retail sales; is an impressive and eye catching presentation of merchandise that attracts shoppers as they pass by your store. Encouraging sales through creative visual merchandise displays is the key to keeping a customer interested in your store.

Chapter Three

Challenges Facing Visual Merchandisers

Visual Merchandising display is the science of displaying merchandise in a retail store and storefront in a bid to increase footfall in a retail store. Besides your store design, visual merchandise display is the best and most effective form of promoting your store.

The most important element of visual merchandising display is that it is on the spot adverting. If a shopper sees a product on display that they like; they can make a purchase immediately and you can make a sale on the spot.

The most important aspect of your visual merchandising display process is in the message. It has to be clear and consistent. When the message is clear, it eliminates the possibility of appealing to the wrong target market and providing a bad customer experience.

Getting your display right is critical for the success of your business. Your display must reflect the quality and price of the products on sale. If you sell high a quality product, but your store design and merchandise display do not match the high end clientele you are intent on attracting, you will lose your target market.

By the same token, if your store appears high end but you sell low qualify products; you will scare off your target market. Consequently, it is essential that you ensure that your display speaks clearly and unambiguously to your target market.

Creativity and the love of design are the two essential requirements for becoming a good visual merchandiser. As a visual merchandiser you need to have the ability to come up with creative ideas about how you would like your display to look.

You need to be a good story teller with a kid like imagination. You need to stay current about developments in your sector and stay in touch with other visual merchandisers to stay abreast of the latest trends.

Challenges visual merchandisers face

Visual merchandisers face a number of challenges that limit their ability to create displays that woo shoppers in to a store. A good visual merchandising display strategy can result in increased sales, increased staff productivity and reduced shrinkage which eventually lead to increased profit.

However, getting visual merchandising right can be a mammoth task for most retail organisations.

The dynamic of the target market is one of the greatest challenges facing visual merchandisers. The volatility of consumer behaviour creates a nightmarish scenario for visual merchandisers who have to constantly invent creative ways to attract potential customers' attention.

The constant development of new products, scarcity of display space allocation and the constant change in consumer preferences all add to the challenging environment for visual merchandisers.

Below is an outline of a few of the challenges that visual merchandisers face:

Too much new merchandise

Figure 13: New products are produced every single day

New products are produced every day. This is a nightmare for visual merchandisers who are responsible for finding display space on the shop floor for new merchandise. The merchandising of fabric is not as difficult as groceries.

Because clothing is seasonal. At the end of each season, clothes belonging to the past season are either sold off or taken to the warehouse. However, the same cannot be said of groceries.

Tones of new products are produced every single day and the supermarket tests most products to see if they will resonate with consumers. It is the work of the visual merchandiser to ensure that each new product is given a space in the store and are visible enough for customers to notice.

This can be a nightmarish scenario especially if it is a low value or bulky product. Placing low value products in high traffic areas is a waste of space. In the same token placing new products in locations where they are not very visible reduces the chances of them being sold. Striking a balance between visibility and space allocation is a huge challenge for visual merchandisers.

Solution

One way of dealing with this challenge is to:

Reserve a specific section of the store for testing products. The only products that will be displayed in this section would be new products. This would make it easy for both visual merchandisers and customers.

If customers are aware that a particular section of the store is specifically reserved for new products, adventure seeking customers would go straight there to look for new products. It also makes it easy for the retailers to quickly gauge customer reaction to the product.

If a product placed there is sold out quickly, the retailer just as quickly recognise the need to order additional supplies fast; and can now move the display to a permanent location in the store. When a new product is placed amongst other products, it can sometimes be difficult to get an accurate picture of its popularity; due to its lack of exposure.

If it is a clothing store, again a specific section of the store can be exclusively set aside for new fashion. Imagine the response that you would receive from customers. They will visit the store specifically to look for the latest fashion.

The creation of such section for new fashion trends will now be multi-purpose: it would serve as a testing lab for new trends; it would provide convenience for customers because they will be able to find things easily and it would serve as a magnet for attracting customers who are bent on keeping up with latest trends.

VISUAL MERCHANDISE: HOW TO CREATE A BEAUTIFUL YET PROFITABLE DISPLAY

Limited Display Space

Figure 14: Retail space is expensive; therefore, every inch of the store's display space needs to be maximised

Retail space is expensive; therefore, every inch of the store's display space has to be used to its maximum. However, with the constant introduction of new products, even hyper stores struggle for space to accommodate all the new products.

To cluster products in a bid to create more space is never a good idea as the store would appear untidy. Even in a store where clothes are replaced seasonally, there are still lots of new fashions that constantly come on the market. Therefore, it really is a struggle for visual merchandisers to decide which clothing or product to give priority in the display.

Solution

The best solution would be to place as much variety as possible but in small quantities. Staff need to keep a constant watch on shelves to ensure that they are not empty or well faced up. If it is a clothing store, the same rule applies. As staff walk around the store, they need to keep their eyes open for empty hangers and spaces between clothes. Every space needs to be immediately refilled.

If it is in a grocery, products also need to be displayed in small quantities. However, the aim has to be to display as much products as possible. Staff need to ensure that no shelf is left empty. The retailer needs to assign a specific supervisor whose job it would be to walk the store every hour checking all shelves and fill gaps as they notice them.

Supplier demand Premium Spacing

Figure 15: Suppliers compete for prominent and high traffic display space

Suppliers compete to have their products displayed in the most prominent and high traffic locations in the store. Here you must be on alert for signs of a conflict of interest between senior management; visual merchandisers and other staff.

The decision as to where products are displayed is often determined by senior management and the supplier; not by the visual merchandiser. Sometimes, what the senior management view as appropriate could prove difficult for visual merchandisers to implement. These conflicting interests result in lack of coordination and cooperation.

In retail, suppliers pay for their products to be displayed in store. There are locations in each store that are considered premium areas: they are mostly high traffic areas. Every supplier wants their products to be displayed in those areas because of a higher probability of increased sales.

And suppliers are will to pay handsomely for the privilege. The problem is sometimes their products contrast with the rest of the products in the department and fitting in their products might reduce the space availability for other products.

Solution

Suppliers and retail senior management need to be educated on the function of visual merchandising display in a retail store. This would help them to make an informed decision about the location of products in the store. Visual merchandising display is showbiz.

The objective is to:

- Attract shoppers as they pass by the store
- Entice them to enter the store
- Retain them for longer in the store
- Persuade them to buy

In order to achieve the above objectives, the placement of products on the shop floor has to be purposefully done, not done haphazardly to favour a few products.

Product security

Figure 16: Product security is very essential

Retail crime; including shoplifting, is responsible for the demise of most retail ventures. Years ago, shoplifting was done by the homeless and drug addicts who wanted to feed their habits.

Currently, shoplifting is conducted by organised retail crime gangs using sophisticated methods never before seen in the retail industry. Retail is a business and business is about making profit. In order to make a profit, a retailer has to increase sales and reduce shrinkage.

One of the best ways of reducing shrinkage is through creative merchandising that does not facilitate the easy pilfering of products from the store. It is therefore essential that visual merchandisers know their role in loss prevention and shrinkage management. The objective of visual merchandising is to attract customers. However, there has to be a balance between attracting customers and protecting products on the shop floor. It is therefore vital for visual merchandisers to be trained in and kept up-to-date with the basics for linking visual merchandising with loss prevention.

If products are displayed with loss prevention in mind, it becomes more difficult for them to be easily removed from the store. However, if the loss prevention aspect of the process is not taken into consideration, the products are at risk when they are placed on the shop floor.

The changing retail environment

Figure 17: The changing retail environment

The internet has removed the monopolization of the factors of distribution once held by a few. In the new retail environment, an individual can run a multi-million pound retail operation from the back of his car as long as he has an internet connection.

It also means that a small factory owner operating from his spare bedroom in China can now compete with a multi-national retail organisation in the West. As it stands, the retail environment demands a different approach to visual merchandising display.

You can no longer continue to view visual merchandising display as just another component of your operation. Visual merchandising along with store design needs to be considered a key component of a retail operation.

Visual merchandising is free advertising for your store. However, despite the fact that it is free; in order for it to be effective, all the fundamentals of advertising need to apply.

In his book "Breakthrough Advertising" Eugene Schwartz wrote "This is the core of advertising—its fundamental function: To take an unformulated desire, and translate it into one vivid scene of fulfilment after another; to add the appeal of concrete satisfaction after satisfaction to the basic drive of that desire. To make sure that your prospect realizes everything that he is getting—everything that he is now leaving behind him—everything that he may possibly be missing"

Below is a list of the fundamental principles of advertising:

- "The only purpose of advertising is to make sales. It is profitable or unprofitable according to its actual sales. It is not for general effect. It is not to keep your name before the people. It is not primarily to aid your other salesmen. Treat it as a salesman. Force it to justify itself. Compare it with other salesmen. Figure its cost and result. Accept no excuses which good salesmen do not make. Then you will not go far wrong".
- "Human nature is perpetual. In most respects it is the same today as in the time of Caesar. So the principles of psychology are fixed and enduring. You will never need to unlearn what you learn about them".
- "Use pictures only to attract those who may profit you. Use them only when they form a better selling argument than the same amount of space set in type".
- "Changing people's habits is very expensive. A project which involves that must be seriously considered. To sell shaving soap to the peasants of Russia one would first need to change their beard wearing habits. The cost would be excessive".

- "Prevention is not a popular subject, however much it should be. People will do much to cure trouble, but people in general will do little to prevent it".
- "We must learn what a user spends a year, else we shall not know if users are worth the cost of getting".
- "We must learn the percentage of readers to whom our product appeals. We must often gather this data on classes. The percentages may differ on farms and in cities".
- "Competition must be considered. What are the forces against you? What have they in price or quality as well as claims to weigh against your appeal? What must you do, to win trade against them? What must you do to hold trade against them when you get it? How strongly are your rivals entrenched"?
- "Almost any question can be answered, cheaply, quickly and finally, by a test campaign. And that's the way to answer them — not by arguments around a table. Go to the court of last resort — the buyers of your product".
- "Consumers all over the world still buy products which promise them value for money, beauty, nutrition, real relief from suffering and social status".

How to Resolve Visual Merchandisers Challenges

The following steps can help to bring relief to visual merchandisers:

1. Make effective use of a planogram to address the challenges of constant new product flow into the market.
2. Study your target market very well to determine product preference.
3. Group products according to make, model and size to enable easy display.

4. Ensure high ticket products are given priority in the display process.
5. Create an illusion of display with a few products that appear to be a lot.
6. Display smaller numbers of each product, especially slow moving products and ensure you make maximum use of the display space allocated.

Chapter Four

How To Burst The Price Myth With Creative Merchandise Display

I visited Harrods for research for this book and my book on store design. Harrods, for anyone reading this book who might not know, is the Mecca for retailing. Royalty, A-list celebrities and the 'who's who' from around the world fly into London just to shop at Harrods.

You can now imagine my anticipation when I visited Harrods. In my mind everything in Harrods was made of gold. I was disappointed; when I noticed a toy bus I had purchased for my son from Asda, was also being sold in Harrods. It was exactly the same toy bus, in exactly the same packaging as the toy in Asda.

A question popped into my mind: why is it that exactly the same bus, probably manufactured in exactly the same factory in China, is sold in Harrods for twice the price that it is sold for in Asda?

> *The answer is decisively simple – Asda sells a 'toy bus, but Harrods sells a 'classy toy bus'.*

There is a difference.

This is marketing 101: people buy emotionally but justify their decision logically.

Customers who shop at Harrods do not shop there to buy Harrods' products; they shop at Harrods to buy 'elegance and class.' Harrods sells them class.

VISUAL MERCHANDISE: HOW TO CREATE A BEAUTIFUL YET PROFITABLE DISPLAY

Figure 18: Harrods customers buy 'elegance and class'

How do Harrods pull this off?

They achieve it with the combination of an elegant store design and attractive visual merchandising displays. When you move from one department to the next in Harrods, it is like moving from one store to another.

Their ability to use their store design to create the illusion of variation is one of the keys to Harrods' success. Harrods understand their customers; they know what their customers want so they design their store and display their products to satisfy the desires of their customers.

The common myth in the retail industry is that people buy more when merchandises are cheap. That is just a myth. In this new retail environment where the monopoly of the factors of distribution has been broken, no retail store can be cheaper than the internet. Even pound stores are not cheaper than the internet.

The main reason people still visit retail stores is either for convenience or to actually feel the products before purchasing them. Some people might visit a retail store just for the fun of shopping.

It is true that 30-40% of people will buy on the basis of price only. However, the large majority of people still buy on the basis of value and convenience.

I am a one click buyer in Amazon. I buy a lot of books because of my line of work. I was pleasantly surprised to learn that I could even buy white board and all my stationary from Amazon.

I cannot remember the last time that I entered a bookstore. I have a lot of friends like me who do the majority of their shopping on the internet. They shop for clothes and even groceries on the net.

Why would I and many of the people do our shopping over the internet?

We are sold on the convenience.

These days there are people who will check things up on the internet, but before placing an order on line; they visit a retail store to see how they look.

The 18th century was about speed of production in order to increase capacity. The 19th century focused on quality. With the increased in production leading to over capacity, the focus shifted from speed to quality.

In the 21st century the focus has shifted from quality to value and total customer experience. But many retailers have failed to grasp the concept.

> Here is the secret, despite the fact that people conduct research on the internet, the large majority still don't trust information found on the internet.

That is why books are still highly rated even though the information in most books can be found on the internet.

People still trust other people and prefer to interact with people. So despite the internet, bricks and mortar retailing will still survive. However, there is a new dynamic and retailers need to understand this.

The consumer of today is better informed than the consumer of ten or twenty years ago. Consequently, today's retail staff need to be better informed than retail staff of ten or twenty years ago.

One cannot navigate the 21st century with a 19th century skill set – it will not work.

Richer Sounds a UK based electronic and entertainment retailer has been featured in the Guinness Book of Records for the past 20 years as having the highest sales per square foot of any retailer in the world.

Coincidentally, their staff continue to top the 'Which" survey for excellent customer service and product knowledge. They are not necessarily the cheapest entertainment retailer in the world but they are the most profitable. Why? Because of the total customer experience that customers receive when they visit their stores.

Since the economic crisis, many middle or low tier retail stores have gone bust or struggling to survive. Yet the luxury sector of the retail market remains buoyant.

Even in recession hit Greece and Spain, the luxury retail market continues to flourish. The explanation that most people would have for this is that the rich are getting richer.

Even though this might be true, this is not the main reason for the continuous buoyancy of the luxury retail market.

The explanation lies in the fact that luxury retailers take the concept of total customer experience to the extreme.

When you visit Harrods, there is staff within an arm's length of each and every customer. On the other hand when you visit some retail stores, you can hardly find anyone to speak to when you need help.

I know of retailers in the UK who advertise on billboards in prime locations around the country. However, when shoppers visit their stores, they can hardly find a staff member to serve them and those in the store might have absolutely no knowledge about the products in the store.

To succeed in the 21st century retail environment, it is the little things that make the difference. As a retailer if you still believe that price is what is going to entice people to your store and make you successful, you are on the wrong end of the stick. 21st century retail is about value and total customer experience.

So as a retailer your focus needs to be on value drive strategies. An essential component of a value driven strategy is an attractive visual merchandising display. As Michael Porter puts it, "cutting prices is usually insane if the competition can go as low as you can".

Maintaining pricing integrity can be challenging in the face of fierce competition. But it can turn out to be a smart business decision in the long run. The concept of value is perceptive.

What might constitute value to one person might not be that valuable to another. However, there is a universal perception about value that exists in the mind of every customer: *cheap is poor quality and expensive is high quality.*

Despite the fact that this concept has proven time and time again to be untrue, like most things in life, it is the perception that matters.

Below is a list of the pricing strategies currently been used by retailers?

Price-matching guarantee

Price-matching guarantee is mostly used by consumer and industrial retailers. Retailers using price-matching guarantee frequently state that they are the 'lowest' priced store, and they will match the competitors.

A store with price matching guarantee will not lose customers to price cuts from other retailers even if it charges higher price to its loyal customers. Price-matching guarantee is an anti-competitive tactic that warns competitors not to attempt to steal market share by undercutting price.

Price slashing

Price cutting is a price strategy used by retailers such as Wal-Mart under their so-called "rolling back prices" price technique to eliminate competition. The core of the strategy is to reduce prices to a level low enough to eliminate competition.

Retailers use this strategy to under-cut the competition and offer the best price to the consumer. The objective is not to sell at a loss, but to reduce price to a point that competition is unable to compete.

Discounting

Discounting is a pricing strategy favoured by most retailers. It is done in the form of coupons, advanced purchases, loyalty cards or bulk buying. Coupons and promotions give buyers an incentive to buy from certain retail stores.

For some customers taking advantage of discount offers can be an attractive proposition. However, for the retailer concerned, discounting of products is never a smart business strategy as it eats into their profit margin.

The following are steps that prevent the need for product discounting:

Step One

Identify and understand your target market.

Like in the case of Harrods, customers visit a particular store for a reason. Your job is to find out who your customers are and what they want.

Step Two

Instead of discounting your current line, you could consider resizing.

As an alternative to discounting their menu, Quiznos took to a decision to resize its sandwiches.

Thus it offered a lower price for the smaller size. Probably there are ways that you could repackage your products in ways that it makes financial sense to discount without eating into your profit margin.

Step Three

Emphasize benefits of the products instead of the price. There is no getting away from the fact that it is very difficult to differentiate one commodity from the other. But it can be done if the retailer places emphasis on other intangible aspects of the buying decision.

Step Four

Emphasize the soft aspect of your offering such as great customer service, knowledgeable staff, easy access to merchandise, easy to locate merchandise or an easy to navigate store.

This might sound trivial, but in marketing, it is the things that are overlooked that count. The everyday thing that you think might not be important to the customer may well be what is really important to them.

The price discounting game is a losing one, do not play it, it is not a good business strategy.

When developing your pricing strategy you need to analyse the market place for sensory acuity. It can be done through the following means:

Competitive analysis

Conduct a competitive analysis of the pricing structure of your competition. When analysing your competitor's prices, your focus should not only be on the amount they charge but also their offering. You need to examine their entire service provision to be able to make an accurate assessment of the reason behind their pricing structure.

Maintain the ceiling price

If you decide to go for the highest price point, ensure it is the ceiling price. The ceiling price is the maximum price the market can bear. It is the price point that if you went above, you might scare away your customers.

Be aware that the price that might be the highest price currently in the market may not be the ceiling price.

Adhere to price elasticity

Price elasticity gives the percentage change in quantity demanded in response to a one percent change in price.

Price elasticity is almost always negative. Only goods which do not conform to the law of demand have a positive PED.

In most cases, the demand for goods is said to be inelastic when the PED is less than one. What this means is that changes in price have a relatively small effect on the quantity of the goods demanded.

The demand for goods is said to be elastic when the PED is greater than one. This means that changes in price have a relatively large effect on the quantity of goods demanded. As you develop your pricing structure, pay attention to these fundamental principles.

The following are steps for implementing an effective pricing strategy; when setting your prices to avoid selling at a loss:

Step One
Determine you cost
Calculate the cost of the product and add corresponding overheads such as: rent, utility bills, staff salary and benefits, marketing, credit cards or bank fees and professional fees.

Step Two
Know competitors prices
After calculating your cost, you then need to check out your competitor's prices for similar products. It comes down once again to ceiling price. If you notice that your price is lower than that of your competition, you will want to check out their offering before drawing conclusions.

On the other hand, if your price is higher, you cannot just reduce your price to match your competitors and operate at a loss. You also need to check out their offering and supply chain.

It is possible that despite the fact that their price is lower than yours, your offering might be more valuable than theirs. If that is the case, you need to ensure that your marketing stresses the fact that your offering is better.

You also need to pay close attention to their supply chain. The reason most grocery retailers struggle to compete with the likes of Wal-Mart and Tesco is because they have stronger bargaining powers when negotiating with suppliers.

This makes it possible for them to drive down their prices. So maybe instead of attempting to go head to head with to bigger players in your market who have strong bargaining powers, you can try changing your offering.

Step Three
Know thy customers

If you understand your customers better than your competitors, you will know the types of price they can bear. Again it is not about the cost of the product; it is about the total customer experience when they enter your store.

Harrods sell the same made in China products, however, it is able to sell it twice the prices of other retailers in the UK because its customers do not only buy at Harrods because of the products, but also because of Harrods total customer experience.

Step Four
Take the market into consideration

It is the market that sets the final price. Your final price would be determined by what the market can bear. The best strategy for testing the market is to start at the highest possible price point.

If you notice that sales are not being made as a result of your price point, you reduce the price and test again. Continue the process until you arrive at a pricing equilibrium.

As you test your prices, ensure that you have an accurate system in place for measuring the result of your pricing test.

How to handle price wars

Price wars are common place in retail. As stated previously, price is the most common strategy for differentiation in retail. Prior to deciding on your course of action during or even before engaging in price wars, you first need to consider this question:

Is the current price of the competition a short-term promotional strategy or a long-term pricing strategy?

If after analyzing your competitor's pricing strategy you reach the conclusion that it is just a short-term promotional strategy instead of log-term pricing strategy, you can either choose to ignore it or develop your own short-term strategy to counter theirs.

On many occasions, a price war is declared because retailers fail to analyse their competitors pricing strategy well.

Below is a list of possible responses to a price war:

Reduce price

You can choose to reduce your own prices in response to the competition's pricing strategy. This would seem on the surface the most logical action to take, but doing so would result in reduction of your profit margin.

Maintain price

You could ignore your competitor and maintain your current pricing strategy and hope that your competitor has made a mistake. This is a risky strategy because if in the process your competitor manages to lure your customers into their store, there is no telling that they would return to your store when the price war is over.

Use split market pricing strategy

This strategy is basically using different price point for similar products. This can be done by restructuring your product offer to promote a certain aspect of the product as basic and another part as premium.

Change your offering

The most effective way of winning a price war is to change your offer and service provision. Providing additional services such as home delivery or free shipment can increase the value of your offering tremendously.

How to implement a value driven strategy?

The best antidote in a price driven market such as retail is to focus on a value driven strategy instead of a price driven strategy. As I pointed out in the case of Harrods and the luxury retail market that is flourishing despite the economic downturn, price is never a good differentiator; therefore it is imprudent for it to be used as a long-term business strategy.

In this 21st century customer centrist environment where the definition of value has shifted from seller to the customer; where competition is fierce and the monopolisation of the factors of distribution has been broken, leaving the field wide open for anyone to enter; success as a retailer would no longer be dependent on 19th century marketing strategies.

> *Succeeding in the 21st century retail requires rethinking your approach to services provision.*

It is now about providing sustainable, durable, reliable and high quality products at reasonable price.

Thousands of retailers are going bust while a few are succeeding beyond their wildest imagination. The retailers that are succeeding understand that the 21st century customer is better informed than customers of the last few decades.

They understand that succeeding in the 21st century retail environment requires a different approach. As a retailer, if your desire is to succeed in the 21st century retail environment, your best course of action should be to update your current operational processes to reflect the realities of the new retail environment.

Below is a list of quality improvement processes used by the most successful companies in the world. Adapting these into your current modus operandi would bring your retail organisation in touch with the realities of the new retail environment.

Hoshin Kanri

Hoshin Kanri or policy deployment; is Japanese for strategically capturing and strengthening strategic goals and developing the means to bring the goals into reality.

Hoshin translated from Japanese to English means shining metal compass, or pointing the direction and Kanri means management or control. As the name suggests using Hoshin planning aligns an organisation toward focusing on the accomplishment of a single goal.

It is a strategic planning and strategic management methodology based on the concept that each person is an expert in his or her own job.

Japanese TQC (Total Quality Control) is designed to use the collective thinking power of all employees to make their organization the best in its field.

This concept was made popular in Japan by Professor Kaoru Ishikawa. In his book "What is Total Quality Control" he asserts that senior and middle managers need to be bold enough to delegate as much authority as possible.

Professor Ishikawa's also believes that a sure way to establish respect for humanity is to adopt management system in which all employees top to bottom participate in the decision making process.

Hoshin Kanri's real aim is to help companies:

- Create common goals
- Communicate those goals to every employee
- Involve all employees in the planning and execution of the plan for achieving the goals
- Create a mechanism for accountability for every participant

Kaizen

Kaizen is Japanese for continuous improvement or change for the better. It is a philosophy that focuses on continuously improving any process.

It can be applied to any work process whether it is manufacturing, engineering, sport, government, healthcare, banking and any on-going activity.

The main objective of kaizen is to eliminate waste and create a benchmark for constantly moving up from one stage to the next.

Kaizen is originally a Buddhist term which comes from the words "renew the heart and make it good".

The adoption of the Kaizen concept in any business demands a change in the very 'heart' of a corporate culture and structure. Kaizen requires businesses to intertwine their vision with every aspect their operational practices.

Kaizen gradual step-by-step process of improving every aspect of a business while at the same time developing employee skills through training and increased participation in the process.

The key areas Kaizen can be implemented in a retail environment are:

- Shop floor – GENBA,
- Product – GENBUTSU
- Training – GENJITSU

By pursuing improvements in the three 'GENs', a retailer is able to spot issues as they arise and can gradually make changes to the key operations – product, service and total customer experience.

Poka-Yoke

Poka-yoke is Japanese for mistake prevention or "mistake-proofing". A poka-yoke is any mechanism that helps a worker avoids mistakes.

The main objective of poka-yoke is to eliminate mistakes by taking preventative and corrective actions prior to an error occurring. Poka-yoke was adopted as a modus operandi by Shigeo Shingo of Toyota as a part of the Toyota Production System.

The fundamental of poka-yoke is to design behavior-shaping constraints into the working process, to prevent incorrect activities by employees.

Below is a list of ways of triggering the thinking process for improving your retail organization:

- The needs of the customer
- It is possible to improve anything
- Quality is the responsibility of all employees
- The employee assigned to a particular job knows more about the job than management
- People should be respected
- Teamwork is critical for success
- Differences should be respected
- Participation in results and commitment

➤ Support results in success

➤ Every employee makes the difference

This book is about visual merchandising so why have I taken the trouble of including information on price and quality improvement. As I have reiterated continuously, the 21st century retail environment is a new environment.

The old modus operandi of previous centuries will not work in the 21st century retail environment. To succeed in retail in this century demands a change from the old way of working.

Visual merchandising has always been perceived in terms of the design and presentation of products. The 21st century visual merchandiser needs to understand the reason behind the process and 21st century senior retail management needs to understand the bigger picture of visual merchandising.

It is no longer just about the presentation of products. It is the thinking process behind the presentation of products that matters the most.

Chapter Five

The Best Merchandise Display Strategy

Shelves and display spaces are the most valuable spaces in a retail store. Consequently, retailers tend to work hard to ensure they maximise return on investment on each square foot of store space.

They display as many products as possible to ensure the maximum utilisation of their display space. Displaying too many products can result in wastage, while displaying too few could result in loss of sales.

The trick is to strike the balance between the two: ensuring customers are able to easily find the products they went into the store to buy and in the process reducing shrinkage.

Visual merchandising display is basically the physical presentation of products for the purpose of increasing sales. Visual merchandising is essential for maintaining the balance between shelf and warehouse stock.

Visual merchandising display is commonly referred to as the silent salesman because a good display effectively sells the products.

The core objectives of visual merchandising are to:

- Enable shoppers to closely examine products
- Maintain the customer's interest in the product
- Encourage them to lower their psychological defences
- Make the purchasing decision easy

However, the most successful retailers do not view visual merchandising as just the display of products on the shop floor. They see it as a marketing tool.

Because they view visual merchandising as a marketing tool, when creating a display, they do not only focus on the physical aspect of placing the products on the shop floor or storefront, they focus on all aspect of the process.

In fact their main focus is on the thinking behind the process rather than the actual process of displaying the products. I will diverge here a little to make this point clearer.

I do a lot of internet marketing, for that I attend lots of internet marketing events taught by the most successful internet marketers in the world. In event after event that I have attended or bought, I continued to observe an interesting trend; the most successful internet marketers do not teach people how to succeed on the internet. Instead they teach marketing fundamentals.

The way they see it, like visual merchandising, the internet is only a vehicle through which they can apply timeless marketing fundamentals. The likes of Google, Facebook, YouTube, Amazon, eBay and many of the successful internet success stories are not successful because their ability to use the internet better than their competitors. They are successful because they applied timeless marketing principles using the internet as an instrument.

There is similar situation with social media. The myth goes that social media can generate loads of customers. As the most successful internet marketers know, social media does not bring anyone business or customers.

It only effective use is to draw traffic to a business's website, the business has to apply timeless marketing principles if it intend on converting those visitors into customers.

The principles of marketing like any principle have never changed. The application might change but the principle itself endures for ever. The fundamentals of marketing have never changed since the beginning of time because human behaviour has never changed since the beginning of time.

This is what one of the world's legendary marketing gurus Eugene Schwartz had to say about this point.

> "Human nature is perpetual. In most respects it is the same today as in the time of Caesar. So the principles of psychology are fixed and enduring. You will never need to unlearn what you learn about them…Consumers all over the world still buy products which promise them value for money, beauty, nutrition, real relief from suffering and social status".

Marketing is what determines the success and failure of any business. Your ability to acquire and retain customers at the most cost-effective rate would determine your level of success in your retail business.

In Value Migration, Adrian Slywotzky stated that:

> "A business (model) design is the totality of how a company selects its customers, defines and differentiates its offerings (or responses), defines the tasks it will perform itself and those it will outsource, configures its resources, goes to market, creates utility for customers and captures profits. It is the entire system for delivering utility to customers and earning a profit from that activity".

In their paper "while the term 'business model' is often used these days, it is seldom defined explicitly." Chesbrough and Rosenbloom point out that there are six specific functions of a business model:

- *Articulate the value proposition – the value created to users by using the product.*
- *Identify the market segment – to whom and for what purpose is the product useful; specify how revenue is generated by the firm.*
- *Define the value chain – the sequence of activities and information required to allow a company to design, produce, market, deliver and support its product or service.*
- *Estimate the cost structure and profit potential – using the value chain and value proposition identified.*
- *Describe the position of the firm with the value network – link suppliers, customers, counterparts and competitors.*
- *Formulate the competitive strategy – how will you gain and hold your competitive advantage over competitors or potential new entrants.*

Joan Magretta wrote in the Harvard Business Review in May 2002:

"A good business model answers Peter Drucker's age-old questions. Who is the customer? And what does the customer value? It also answers the fundamental questions every manager must ask. How do we make money in this business? What is the underlying economic logic that explains how we can deliver value to customers at an appropriate cost"?

As you make plans for your visual merchandise display I want you to give some thought to the above messages. The main objective of a visual merchandise display is to motivate customer interest in your products. Displays should also be able to provide information about the products; show customers how to use the product.

A good visual merchandise display strategy answers the following questions:

- Does the display fit your brand image?
- Is it attractive enough to capture the customers' attention?
- Does it have a story to tell to the customer?
- Does it have a clear and specific message for the customer?
- Is it focused on the product?
- Is the information of the display easy to read?
- Does the lighting system bring out the best in the display?
- Is the display well organised?

The answers to the above questions will result in:

- Increase footfall
- Increased impulse buying
- Good brand positioning
- Effective use of display space allocation

In the fiercely competitive retail market you need to ensure you provide your customers the total shopping experience they crave. Taking the time to think through your merchandise display process – applying fundamental marketing principles will provide you huge competitive advantage over your competitors.

What is a good merchandise display strategy?

So how can you influence your customer or potential customers' buying decision through the creative use of a visual merchandise display? You can do that by simply asking yourself:

What catches your attention and persuades you to enter a particular store amongst three hundred stores in a shopping centre?

An answer to this question would bring you closer to answering the question of how to influence your customer's buying decision.

A creative visual merchandise display must have the following:

Balance

Balance refers to the manner in which the products are arranged around an imaginary centerline. When the phrase formal balance is discussed in relation to a visual merchandise display, this means that a product is on one side of the line, and a similar product is displayed at the same distance from the line between both products in the display. Balance encompasses the symmetry and weight of products on two sides of a display.

Emphasis

Emphasis is using one product in the display as the centre of attraction. The product would be core of the display around which the rest of the display is arranged.

The emphasis in a display is where the potential customer is expected to look first and it is deliberately arranged by the visual merchandiser to be the most prominent component of the display. All good visual merchandise displays have an emphasis.

Proportion

Proportion is the dimension and spacing of products in a display. Proportion can refer to the relationship between the product used as emphasis and the rest of the products in the display.

When the word proportion is used in relation to a merchandise display, it refers to the relative association of every piece of the display in relation to the: distance, size, amount and degree of differentiation.

Rhythm

Rhythm is the measurement of systematised movement from one product to the next in a merchandise display. Rhythm is an inexplicit guide tactically placed in the display to guide the customer's eyes from product to product in the display back to front and/or side to side.

The rhythm is also necessary for leading the eyes of the customer from the product of emphasis to the rest of the products on display as they look at them.

Harmony

Harmony conveys the mood and emotions of the display. It is obviously the most important aspect of the display. However, because it is not a tangible object, its essence could be lost in the display. Harmony is the story and message within the products on display. It is what brings the display to life and gives it character.

There are self-service and full-service displays

Self-Service

The Self-service display is a display in which the products on display are the ones on sale. If customers see a product in the display that they like, they can select the product and take it to the checkout counter.

Full-Service

A full-service display on the other hand is a mock display of the products. The main products are kept in the warehouse or behind the customer services counter. If customers see a product in the display that they like, they need to call one of the store associates who will go and collect the product for them.

This sort of display is usually used for expensive or large products and it is frequently used in luxury and upscale retail environments.

Big retailers often use a combination of both self-service and full-service.

How to conduct a good merchandise display strategy

The two types of displays are window and interior displays.

Window Display

Window displays are merchandises displayed in the shop window to attract shoppers as they pass by the store. The main objectives of a window display is to attract shoppers attention and entice them to enter the store.

Consequently, window displays are often brightly and impressively colored and lit. Window displays are usually season and occasion related; for example a window display for Valentines would be done in red and white colours and hearts reflecting love.

Interior Display

An interior display as the name suggests is the display of merchandise inside the store. Interior displays are also strategically located in various locations of the store to attract customers' attention as they move from one part of the store to the next.

The main objectives of interior display are to increase customer desire for the merchandise, show what merchandises are available, and stimulate both impulse and planned buying.

There are three types of interior displays: Open; closed, and Point-of-Purchase.

Open Display

An open display is one in which customers have access to the merchandise. They can touch, feel and try on merchandises in an open display.

Closed Display

Closed displays are displays that restrict customer access. Merchandises are usually kept enclosed in display cabinets and behind the cashier checkout counters.

Point of Purchase Display

Point of Purchase Display refers to products that are displayed close to the checkout counter. The main objective of this display is to encourage impulse buying. The Point of Purchase Display can be used to introduce new products, announce special offers or stimulate "no brainer" purchases such as lip balms, pens and small items.

When planning your visual merchandise display, take the following into consideration:

Your Brand Image

Is the display consistent with your brand image?

As a retailer, you represent a certain image to the public.

That image needs to be reflected in all of your marketing materials, messages and visual merchandise displays.

As you plan your display, the question that needs to be core to the process is, does the design represent the brand image you are known for?

Your target market

The next point that needs to be considered is: does the design appeal to your target market? I am making the assumption that you already know your target market. So as you prepare your design story board, the question that your need to be asking is, does this message speak to our target market?

If the answer is yes, then your display is effective. If no, you will need to tweak it until it speaks directly to your target market.

What's the concept?

What is the concept of the display?

What would it be communicating to your target market?

The most effective displays are the ones in which the products are displayed exactly how they are to be used. It could be a clothing display in which the item is dressed on a mannequin the way someone is expected to wear it or in a furniture store where furniture are arranged in a way that they are expected to be arranged in a room.

The display structure

Considerations have to be given to the area in which the display is to be located. The location of the display has a significant impact on how it is to be designed? In retail store displays are usually located in: windows, walls, cases, gondolas or islands. The specific area in which the display is to be located within the store would determine its size and shape.

Promotional displays

Displays created for promotional purposes need to be different from the rest of the displays in the store. Promotional displays need to be located in the front of the store for a short period after which they should be moved to the back of the store if you intend on carrying on the display for a long time.

Customers who are interested in bargains will find it no matter the area of the store it is located.

Your customers need to be treated to new and exciting displays every week to create a sense of freshness in their heads. Always ensure that you have enough products in stock during promotional periods to cater to customer demand.

The following steps for creating displays that would increase your sales:

Step One
Determine the goal of the display

Every display needs to have a specific goal. The questions with which to determine this are: Is the goal of the display to promote new products; to carry on promotion; to attract a new target market to your store?

There needs to be a goal for each and every display.

Step Two
Choose the right merchandise

The merchandise on display needs to reflect the types of merchandise you sell. To ensure this takes place, the questions you need to answer are:

Does the merchandise on display match the quality of your product?

Does it reflect your brand image?

Your merchandise displays need to contain the right product for the right time. If the display is for Valentine, every product on the display needs to be related to valentine.

Step Three
Choose a theme

Every display needs to have a theme. The theme of the display is the story behind the display. You need to be able to identify the message you want the display to send to your target market. The theme of your merchandising can be a way to communicate a seasonal message to your target market.

Step Four
Select props

Props are the items used in a merchandise display to physically support merchandises that form part of the display theme. Props are essential for strengthening the message of a display.

Prop characters are essential for determining the overall appearance and feel of a display hence the reason why it is essential to get the appropriate props for your display.

Step Five
Create a contextual display

Create contextual displays by merging similar products together. This makes buying decisions easier for customers. For example: putting together shirt and ties or shoes and socks.

When products are grouped together, they make it easier for customers to make their choice. It also results in increased sales as it encourages a lot impulse buying.

Step Six
Develop signs

Ensure your signage is visible enough to complement the merchandise on display. There needs to a balance on the amount of signage placed on a display to avoid confusion.

The objective of signage in a display is to provide information such as the price of the products on display. It needs to be brief and easy to read. Signage should also prompt customers to move around the store. The sign should basically covertly inform that there are more great products to be seen in the store.

Step Seven
Design the lighting

Your lighting system is the most important element of your display. You need to ensure that the lighting system used for your display is the most appropriate one. The lighting system is also very crucial for your display because the right lighting system enhances the appearance of the products.

A good lighting system can also create an illusion and make products in the display appear more valuable than they actually are.

The light should be enough to enable the customer to examine the display and read the signs related to it. You can use a spotlight to highlight specific items in the display.

Ensure the lighting system does not cause glare and shadows around the display area. This is done effectively when you have different lighting sources.

Finally, displays must be neat and simple.

A cluttered display sends a bad impression of your store.

A confusing display would result in poor sales.

Therefore, it is very important that displays are:

- Neat
- Uncluttered
- The display area clean

There are no unrelated things lying about

The objective of the display should be to:

- Attract customers as they pass by the store
- Entice them to enter the store
- Retain them for longer in the store
- Persuade them to buy

Remember visual merchandising display is first and foremost a marketing tool, therefore the design has to be infused with timeless fundamental marketing principles.

Chapter Six

How To Maximise Display Space Allocation With Creative Display

Maximising display space to achieve the maximum return on investment per square foot ought to be a main objective of your visual merchandising display strategy. The cost of retail space by square foot is on the increase. So too is the variation of products. Creative use of display space is particularly relevant for retailers who sell low value products.

There are only so many products that can be crammed on a shelf in a small retail space. This means that space needs to be used creatively, to result in maximum profit for the retailer.

What Is Creative Space Use?

Creative visual merchandise space is the efficient use of retail space to maximise its potential capacity while retaining the sense of present-ability. This allows the products for presentation to appear neat and eye catching to the passing customer.

The efficient use of retail display space has several benefits:

- The ability to stock more products

The more space you have to display merchandise the more products you can display in your store.

- More supplier support

With fierce competition in the retail marketplace, all suppliers want their products to be allocated a space in a store, preferably in the high traffic areas. Consequently, suppliers are willing to bargain for marketing support and higher space rental just to get the space that they want.

- More organised and controlled displays

An organised and well-controlled display area results in the maximisation of space. When your store is well-organised it is easier to monitor your products. There is also less incidents of pilferage and theft.

- Increased consumer satisfaction

Aside from good quality products and services that the store offers, availability is also very important to the consumer. Product prices prove irrelevant in comparison to convenience and quality.

- Increased sales and profit

Increased customer satisfaction results in increased sales and profit. Word of mouth advertisement based on personal experience is the oldest but still the most effective marketing tool.

For example, grocery items displayed on end caps and promotional merchandise situated near the store entrance are more likely to attract customers' attention than if they are positioned in a side aisle or in the back of the store.

- It helps prevent out-of stock and inadvertently lose sales

When you display your merchandise properly on the shop floor, they can be easily monitored by staff to ensure that the spaces are constantly refilled. In most cases when customers notice that a product is not on a display only a few customers who desperately need the item would bother to ask store associates. The majority would just assume that it is unavailable in the store and go somewhere else and buy.

The effectiveness of a visual merchandise display space would depend on a few key factors:

- The type of merchandise you sell
- The location of the building
- Your store design
- The amount you are willing to allocate to the process

Display space allocation is the most complicated challenge facing most retailers. New products are constantly been introduced into the market. As those new products are brought into the store, the visual merchandiser is charged with the responsibility of finding display space for all of the new products.

One-third of the products each year in an average retail, are new products. Each new product brings with it the accompanying challenge of finding a suitable spot on the shop floor.

To ensure an effective use of your display space, take the following into consideration:

Set a realistic budget

The first thing that needs to be taken into consideration is your budget. How much will you realistically spend on visual merchandising; knowing fully well the benefits of the process?

Answering this question would help you set budgetary priorities to ensure you focus your spending on essential elements such as lighting, display area, fixtures, shelving, storage units and furniture as well as floor and wall coverings.

Create a blueprint

A blueprint of your display space taking into consideration you product line is another point to consider when developing your visual merchandising display plan.

You need to monitor your sales volume, price point and profit margin to ensure that you are effectively using your display space. By monitoring your results, you can keep tweaking your blueprint to ensure you are making maximum use of your display space.

Plan the traffic flow

Customers need to be able to properly examine the products from all angles to make an informed buying decision. Ensure you allow sufficient space for aisles and give consideration to the projected traffic flow.

Remember, you would want your customers to move through your display areas and to the checkout counter with ease. Designing customer flow and accessibility into the visual merchandising display blueprint would help make the process smoother.

There are three basic visual merchandising display space structural frameworks:

Open Structure

An open structure enables customer flow from one product to the next without any barriers or obstacles. The open structure enables the separation of space; however it is done in such a way that it does not hinder the movement of customers around the display.

Grid Structure

In the grid structure, products are displayed in enclosed spaces according to product categories. Adequate segregation is provided on every product category. If the store carries a lot of different product categories extensive efforts are made to ensure each product category is well separated from the next.

Boutique Structure

With the boutique structure, products are placed next to each other. This allows the customer the freedom to choose at will. The drawback of this structure is it can be difficult for the customer to navigate through the products.

In retail; space means money. The store has to be designed in such a way that it optimises the selling area and minimises the non-selling areas.

The selling area is used to present the merchandise and the non-selling section is taken up by passage space, aisles, staircases, lifts, facilities, and the back area. The area mix in a usual department store is: selling area about 65%, circulation area 15% and back area 20%.

In a ready-made garment retail store; setting up the size of the selling space starts with a wardrobe audit where a sample size of the customer section is intercepted and their wardrobe mix of garments and accessories planned out.

This will determine the number of styles and the range width of the same category. Then a store design is made based on the space integration. The selling space is then planned in terms of size and place of merchandise and based on the mix of staple, convenience and impulse merchandise.

How to use space well

The display of a good retail store with attractive windows and an inviting entrance attracts the customer to enter. The customer enters the store and often keeps walking inside following the walkway wherever it leads or sometimes takes a while to look for directions within the store. Sometimes the customer's attention is drawn to certain displays and merchandise presentations before he moves on.

Merchandise can be efficiently displayed on a variety of fixtures such as gondolas, tables, cubes, mannequins, waterfalls and other racks. Display cases and manufacturer point-of-purchase displays are also handy.

A fixture should not only match the merchandise, but also the environment created in the store. Each fixture is presenting the merchandise to the public and as such acts as a silent salesperson.

The space must be specially designed for the type of product being sold in that section. For example, a bookstore requires many shelving units to hold some products that can be arranged by category. On the other hand, a clothing store will need more open spaces to fully display all its merchandise. Once within the store, the customer needs to be guided silently to where he/she wants to go and also expose him/her to the entire store offering. This can be achieved by setting up the flow and the location of the merchandise.

The aisles forming a pattern flow can be of different types based on the store arrangement. The section occupied by the aisles is normally 12-15% of the store carpet area.

Below are some types flow layouts you can choose from:

Free Flow
This layout is used in stores where the merchandise and fixtures are grouped in clusters.

Grid Flow
This type is usually used in supermarkets where the aisles and fixtures are at right angles to each other.

Race Track

This is generally utilized in larger and wider stores where the customer is made to circle around the floor and get back to the beginning, usually the lift or the staircase lobby, to move to the next level of the store.

Herringbone Flow

This is used most of the times for a narrow store of at most 40 ft. wide wherein the freeway is a single two-way one, bisecting the store along its length with "side roads' leading to the walls from it.

The proper utilisation of store space will require the retailer to focus on these three important steps simultaneously:

Step One
Get the appropriate space and product assortment

Retailers optimise and rationalise their assortments based on enhanced analysis of profitability and the apprehension that variety may be overwhelming for customers.

They know they need to do a better job of understanding the assortment. So they assume the role of selector and chief buyer on behalf of the consumers. The positions of various goods are chosen carefully to ensure that the customer is exposed to the entire store; thus increasing the possibility of a purchase.

Step Two
Systematize strategies to manage space

Retailers should re-evaluate their business operations; standardise new and revise older formats. They should competently segment and align their retail space to consumer needs and purchasing behavior.

At the same time they should explore other opportunities for growth.

Step Three
Integrate online and offline channels

The increasing importance of online shopping is changing notions of space management. It introduces the concept of the "endless aisle" and encourages retailers to treat the Internet as an integral part of their operations.

The retail business is very competitive, with thousands of contending retail establishments vying for attention, space management does not end with optimisation.

It creates greater opportunity for merchandise promotion and presentation, which will not only result in higher profit margin but also customers retention.

Below are additional important tips for optimising your store space relative to effective utilization of your fixtures:

Use modern fixtures

An article titled "The Psychology of Shopping," looks at retailing nearly four decades ago. It revealed that the retail giants of the 1970s relied heavily on the philosophy of "pile it high; sell it cheap" and they found success with that philosophy.

Although retailers are currently using more sophisticated ways of capturing the attention of shoppers, this philosophy remains pervasive. To successfully compete in the contemporary retail environment requires you change your philosophy along with your fixtures to more modern eye-catching fixtures.

Choose fixture to match your target market

Pick displays and fixtures that are distinctively suited to your target market.

Who is your target market?

What type of customer do you have?

Take a detailed look at your own store. In what ways are the store fixtures and displays matching the types of customers you wish to attract?

Plan your display strategies

Plan your space using display systems that make it trouble-free for your customers.

The width of the aisles needs to be selected according to the density and traffic pattern.

The main aisle or 'highway' in a department store is six feet wide, which is the width of a double doorway. It facilitates easy passage in both directions. The side aisles or 'side roads' that branch out are three or four feet wide.

In supermarkets, the aisles are three feet wide and form a denser grid around the fixtures.

When planning you display space, you need to take into account the following:

- The average person's field of vision tends to be around 170 degrees
- The number of product categories in the store
- The percentage of space to be allotted to each category
- The volume of merchandise in each category
- The relative placement of each category

How to implement good space allocation

The primary purpose of retail space is to stock and sell product to consumers. The spaces must be designed in a way that promotes an enjoyable and hassle-free shopping experience for the consumer.

The shelf space problem is quite different depending on whether we take the perspective of the manufacturer or the retailer.

Manufacturers want to maximise the sales and profits of their products, and as such always want more and better space to be allocated to their brands.

Retailers want to maximize category sales and profits, regardless of brand identity; they must allocate a fixed amount of shelf space in the best possible way.

Here are a few things to consider when allocating display space:

Fixture arrangement

One of the most common fixtures in stores are gondolas – movable shelving that are accessible from all sides.

They should be lined up in rows as in grocery, hardware and drug stores or used singly to form an island.

When placing racks, progress from small fixtures to large fixtures near the back walls. When working with hard goods, place cubes in the front with gondolas to the rear of the department or store.

Higher end stores require fewer fixtures because there are less merchandise. Use primarily T-stands and four ways to create an illusion of space for selective goods.

This is necessary to sell higher ticket products.

Contextual Merchandising

Similar merchandise should be grouped together on the end-cap and gondola sides. The end-cap should indicate the type of related merchandise on the gondola sides. For example, golf balls displayed on an end-cap should indicate that related golf accessories are located on gondola sides.

End-caps are units at the end of aisles. End-caps are important selling fixtures that should be used for high ticket impulse or seasonal merchandise.

Centralise high ticket products

Customers usually look to the center of gondola sides first before looking either to the left or right. Additional high ticket impulse items should be placed in the center of gondola sides and other related merchandise to either the left or right.

Larger more expensive merchandise should be placed to the right.

Furthermore, high ticket items should be placed at eye level.

Allow contact

If possible, remove a sample from packaging to allow customers to touch and feel the items. Old merchandise should be cleaned and pulled forward as new merchandises are added to the display.

Use a starter gap in which at least one item is missing, so the customer will not feel like they are messing up a neat display.

Create rainbow presentation

Make stimulating displays with mass merchandise by using quantity and color. A good way of arranging merchandise on a gondola is by color. People think of colors in a rainbow pattern and are comfortable with that sort of presentation.

Display merchandise in quantity on quads, round and T-stands; use cubes for folded goods.

Restock the display before it gets down to the last item so customers will not get the impression that something is wrong with the item.

If merchandise are broken the remaining items should be moved to the bottom shelves of the gondola.

Use geometric pattern

A well-planned geometric aisle pattern works best to maximize sales. Place aisle displays in an island rather than wing fixtures.

Fixtures that work well for sale items include tub tables, round racks and rectangular rackslay product. Allow need to be three feet between racks.

Leave fire exit free

The aisle leading directly to the fire exit is considered a major aisle. Do not block the fire exit with fixtures or extraneous materials. Legal requirements for aisle width vary from four to eight feet.

The most common aisle width is six feet. Check your local codes for the your local requirements.

Your goal should be to have enough products of display, not overcrowded fixtures and walls. In addition, clearly delineated product categories. Maximising fixture practice requires fresh eyes and a creative spirit alongside a desire to drive sales.

The new representation for retail success includes not only space utilisation but an integrated approach to space management that will drive traffic, increase sales and profitability.

Retailers should understand the changes in consumer behavior and preferences and align their space management strategies accordingly.

Chapter Seven

The Benefits Planogram Software

More and more retailers as well as manufacturers are now using planogram to create images shelf strips, shelf tags and back tags to help store associates produce prompt and accurate visual merchandising display.

A planogram is a marketing instrument used in retail stores. It is an illustration or drawing that provides details of where a product should be placed on a shelf and how many facing that product should be. It is used by a retail store to increase sales and by suppliers to justify the space allocated of brands and new products.

Retailers employ planograms so they come up with product displays that draw customers' interest and help them to sell more products as a result. The complexity of a planogram may differ by the size of store, the software used to create the planogram and the need of the retailer.

Why is planogram good for visual merchandising?

Figure 19: Planogram makes merchandising display easy

As competition heats up; an increasing number of retailers as well as distributors are becoming more aware of the importance of marketing their products. They are beginning to realise that better marketing leads to improved sales.

Planograms are an accurate way of presenting new ideas for product placement, testing merchandising principles and understanding best possible inventory requirements. It is a schematic of shelve and fixture positioning of products on those shelves or fixtures.

Successful retail space planning and management is an important part of the merchandise planning and execution. A well-designed shopping environment catches the attention of customers, prevents stock outs, enhances inventory productivity, reduces operating costs and most of all boosts the financial performance of the store.

Here are the advantages of utilising planogram for visual merchandising:

Guaranteed product placement

Figure 20: Planogram ensures optimum supply chain efficiency

Accurate store-specific planograms ensure optimum supply chain efficiency that results in higher availability to shoppers, maximum stock turn over and the most efficient use of space.

Improved sales

Targeted store-specific planograms direct maximum in-store compliance, resulting in an accurate understanding of product distribution and eventually increase sales.

Tighter inventory control and reduction of stock outs items

Focused store-specific planograms leads to increased sales and profitability, easier product replenishment, reduction in stock and operational costs and an overall enhancement in bottom line contribution.

Satisfying customers with a better visual appeal

Improves customer satisfaction by making it easier to shop in shelves that are well-organised and reduces the time it takes to arrange stock in the store. Influence customer behaviour for trade-up and impulse buying, which result increased sales.

Effective communication tool for staff

Tailors assortments including product launches and group-specific go-to-market strategies so that you can improve cluster results and meet true local demand and effectively communicate with your staff.

Assigned selling potential to every inch of retail space

Enables better management of inventory by allocating shelf space and facings based on movement, which in turn reduces out-of-stocks; streamlines space and floor planning, so that you can increase your space productivity and optimise your capital investment.

Merchandising Tactics

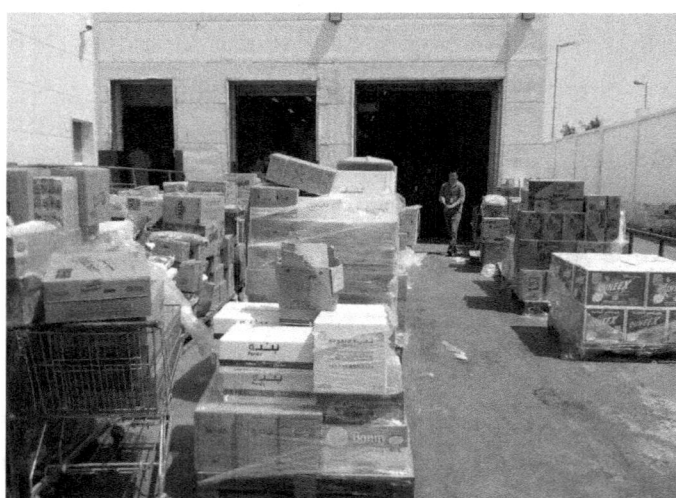

Figure 21: Planogram Enables better inventory management

Improved merchandising best practices by testing and comparison of cause and effect in like stores; translates merchandising strategy into tactics; so that you can drive consistent store execution of your corporate strategic and assortment decisions.

Planograms will give you a good idea of how a display will look before you physically dress that merchandise on to the shelves in your store. This saves you time and ensures you are not frequently distracting and irritating your customers, by always dressing and re-dressing shelves until you find a product layout that works.

Planograms can be as easy as a photo of a preset section or more thorough with numbered peg holes and shelf notches showing exact position of each item.

Planogram diagrams received by a store may be imprecise or worse nearly impractical to implement because the category size, orientation, or shelving in a particular store may not match the planogram.

In some cases, resetting can be hampered by shelf tags and layouts that rely on shortened names.

Product positioning and enhanced sales are just two important reasons why a retailer should be implementing planograms in their stores. Using a planogram helps a retailer design different product layouts and compare them side by side.

Below are some things to consider when implement planogram in your store:

Quality

Includes shelf heights, merchandise placements and the quantity of facings. Shelf heights depend on the volume of the products and ease of reach for the customers.

Merchandise placement illustrates which shelf and where on that shelf a product should be placed. A facing is a row of products. Thus, if a product has two facings, there are two rows of that product on the shelf.

Importance

The arrangement and number of facings merchandise has will considerably change its sales at the store. It will also change the store's overall performance. It is recommended that the product be placed at eye level and have the maximum amounts of facings.

It is significant for the store to let its most profitable products have the most facings and be located at eye level. And avoid wasting space by placing low ticket slow-moving products with low profit margin in premium locations.

Purpose

The objective of the planogram is to increase sales and offer the most popular product the best spot to attract customers. A store should regularly modify the layout of all of its fixtures.

For example, the design of the children formula section in a supermarket will be different every few months depending on what is hot in that period.

The stores use a planogram to make a decision on how the section will look and what merchandise will be most available to the customer. Besides, with each layout of a planogram, the store will make the fixtures appear more aesthetic to the customer.

Time Schedule

Planograms are typically planned a few weeks in advance of its implementation. A company that specializes in planograms and merchandising will design them using specialized software. Then they will be tested on pilot shelves to ensure they are suitable for the store before deploying it.

How Planogram is used

For a chain of retail stores, planogram guarantees the uniformity of product placement at all locations and wholesalers use the sketches to implement the display of their product. In effect, it gives them the highest sales volume.

Independent retailers use planogram to make the best use of shelf space and improve the look of products. Operating with an efficient planogram is one way to ensure products are replenished and maintained in a way that develops the quality of the display.

A good retailer should understand that the key to increased sales is proper merchandising. A planogram is one of the best merchandising tools for presenting products to the customer.

Listed below are the types of commonly used planogram:

Box with text

The most basic form of planograms utilises box shapes to represent to different goods, with the name of the item typed inside the box.

For example, a planogram intended for a noodle aisle might have rows of larger rectangular boxes to packs of instant noodles.

The brand of instant noodles will be written inside of the box. There may be two rows of each brand depending on the store's requirement.

If the store is usually selling more of one brand, there will be more facings of the high seller. These planograms are typically black and white, two-dimensional diagrams intended for use in grocery stores or areas of retail department stores where merchandise are moving fast.

Pictorial

Pictorial planogram is normally used in clothing and department stores wherein displays are more important and arrangement is essential.

Pictorial planograms are more difficult and thorough compared with the basic planograms.

Pictorial planograms include images of the product and how it should be displayed.

It may show how shirts should be arranged on the shelf or it may demonstrate how dishes or small appliances should be displayed. These planograms are generally flat, two-dimensional, computerised illustrations.

They are typically drawn more precisely to scale and are in color to give an exact representation of how the items are to be displayed.

3-D

Planogram application differs by retail sector. Three-dimensional planograms are usually drawn to scale and include aerial views of the area. As technology advances, so to do the applications and software used to create planograms.

The 3-D type includes whole department layout. Computer generated photographic illustrations of how the department, including promotions and displays should appear. These technologies have led to the growing popularity of three-dimensional planograms.

Fast-moving consumer product industry and supermarkets most of the time use text and box based planograms that optimizes shelf space, inventory turns, and profit margins.

Department Stores are more focused on presentation therefore use pictorial planograms that project "the image" and also identify each product.

Factors to consider when implementing planogram that makes the buying process easier for the customer, which simultaneously result in increased sales for the store are:

Planned Category

Customers might need a product but prior to going to the store have not determined which brand, size, quantity and flavour they require. Having planned category help make customer decision easier.

Impulse buying

A customer might not have plans of buying an item, but seeing the item on display might trigger their desire to buy it.

Substitution

An appropriately merchandised planogram can influence trade-up or trade-down purchases. For example, a customer originally plans to purchase Brand 'A' but proper planogramming directs the customer to Brand 'B' which is offered as a better value.

Triggered

The busy customers frequently appear at the store knowing what they want to purchase; they just don't have a specific list. A "triggered" purchase takes place when they see the product on the shelf which serves as a reminder and that encourages them to buy.

Contextual

Making sure that product category is accurately placed through the aid of correct planogramming will lead to larger transactions and happier consumers.

An incremental purchase is completed as a result of purchasing another product. For example, a customer purchases paint and the appropriately arranged planogram reminds them of the need for a brush, tape, and other items needed to perform the task.

One very essential rule of good quality planogramming is "always anticipating the customer's need." Picture strips and tags are well-liked by shoppers because it helps them understand "product-to-price" identification and let customers know that an item is sold even if it is currently out of stock.

How does planogram work?

The goal is to take full advantage of the quantity of merchandise on display and the amount of sales by arranging merchandise in a way that they will look enticing to customers.

Planogram was designed aim of:

- Increasing sales
- Increasing profits
- Creating a proper way of introducing a new product
- Supporting a new merchandising approach

Deviating from the planogram defeats the rationale of any of the above stated goals.

The full benefits of planogram can be best achieved if the following steps are being followed:

Step One
Identify the purpose

Decide product positioning and sales betterment are few reasons why you should implement planogram. Outline the kind of display you plan on implementing.

Step Two
Map out the display

The display cases and shelves are the most important elements of a planogram. Start by illustrating the backdrop and draw as accurately as possible so it can be used literally as instructions for organising your shelves.

Step Three
Organize your merchandise

Try out different ways of arranging your merchandise so that they fit as best as possible and will be easily seen.

Decide where you want the products to be positioned using shapes that have the same dimensions and forms of the actual products.

Step Four
Add Labels

Using labels and product images will give you the absolute feel of what you have arranged. It will also let anyone involved in the planning envisage the display.

Step Five
Implement It

Use the illustration to create the life size display. If all of your dimensions are accurate, you should be confident that everything will fit as you planned.

To fully appreciate the value of planogram, any retailer deciding to implement planogram should first be able to read and understand diagrams.

Here are a few pointers to help you read and understand planogram:

Determine whether you have the appropriate planogram for your store. Some retail chains will have different planograms to accommodate the various sizes of stores.

To ensure you are merchandising the right product, match the bar code on the product with your SKU list. This is a listing of all the products and the number of facings, or the number of times each product is to be merchandised on the shelf.

Most planogram software takes some time to master fully, so start with a small display area in your store which contains only a few lines. Locate the lead-in arrow, in the bottom left corner of the schematic. This shows the direction in which the planogram is to be set.

When implementing planogram it is recommended you allocate space based upon product sales performance. A basic rule of planograming is to ensure there are enough products on the shelf to meet the customer's requirement.

Knowing how to read a planogram is a key component of a successful visual merchandising display strategy. It aids in speeding up product placement on the shop floor and increase performance efficiency.

What can you do in your store right now to implement planogram?

Here are some things to consider when implementing planogram:

Location

Where in the store located?

Are there secondary placements?

Category Space Allocation

How much space will be allocated to each category?

Product Space

What will spaces allocation be based upon: sales, movement, mandates or inventory thresholds?

Layout

How will the planogram be structured based upon: price, brand or manufacturers?

Labels/ Signage

How would the category or section benefit from signage or point of purchase materials?

Planogram makes the work of your employees easy at store level as they do not need to do the thinking about where products are to be placed, increasing staff productivity and decreasing shrinkage.

Chapter Eight

How To Profitably Display Merchandise

London based Harrods is one of the most successful retailer in the world. Royalties, A-list stars and the "Who-is-Who" from around the world fly to London just to shop at Harrods.

What is responsible for Harrods spectacular success?

There are three factors responsible for Harrods phenomenon success…

- Good store design
- Attractive visual merchandise display
- Effective loss prevention strategy

The subject of loss prevention is something that has never been taken seriously by the retail industry even though the industry spends billions every year on loss prevention. In the last ten years loss prevention spending has increased tremendously. In 2011 the total cost of retail crime plus loss prevention was $128 billion; but retail shrinkage rose to $119 billion.

So why is it that despite the huge amount spent on loss prevention, retail shrinkage continues to rise?

To answer this question, I will give you a quick tour of Harrods.

Harrods store design and visual merchandising displays are definitely factors in its success. The key factor to Harrods' success though is its ability to remain profitable. Profit is king in retail. In retail the formula for making profit is to increase sales and reduce shrinkage.

Increasing sales requires a good store design and attractive visual merchandising; whereas reducing shrinkage calls for an effective loss prevention strategy.

This is what Harrods and most successful retailers have over the rest of the retail industry: their ability to simultaneously increase sales and reduce shrinkage. Most retailers know how to increase sales, however, when it comes to reducing their shrinkage, they are challenged.

Getting the two right is the fundamental principle of retail success. No retailer can succeed without simultaneously increasing sales and reducing shrinkage.

Why do shrinkage reduction or loss prevention measures fail in most retail organisations?

Loss prevention measures fail in retail is a result of the following reasons:

- Lack of understanding of the subject
- Senior management's failure to prioritise
- Outsourcing loss prevention without a mechanism for accountability
- Inexperienced loss prevention managers
- Ineffective use of loss prevention technology.

Harrods is the first retail store that I have ever entered that has no visible blind spots. I am not saying that there are absolutely no blind spots as I managed to spot a few.

However, the difference with other stores is that they are not visible to the unprofessional eyes.

Anyone deciding to shoplift in Harrods would have to be:

- A professional shoplifter or part of an organised retail crime syndicate
- Really brave
- Really stupid

Products are displayed in such a manner that each department seems wide open. Store staff can stand at one end of a department and have a clear view of the entire department.

Figure 22: Harrods drastically reduced the possibility of shoplifting

There is CCTV in every corner of the store; in addition store assistants buzzing around like bees make it difficult for anyone who might intend to shoplift.

I will not go as far as to say that it is impossible to shoplift at Harrods; because I know shoplifting prevention requires the implementation of a raft of strategies.

However, by designing their store as they have done; by displaying their products in the manner that they do and by taking loss prevention measures seriously; Harrods have drastically reduced the possibility of shoplifting.

Now contrast Harrods loss prevention strategy with a store in the top ten UK retailers that I once worked for as a store detective.

This was a few years back. On my very first day of work, as I was in the middle of a briefing with the officer I was to relieve, I noticed a couple walk into the store and head for the coat section. I stood there perplexed as I witnessed the lady remove one of the coats from the hanger; put it on and then casually walk to the exit with her partner and scurry into the waiting getaway car.

£900 walked out the door with such incredible ease, making me think "Holy cow! How can this sort of thing happen in broad daylight?"

> *The answer was actually quite apparent: The coats were prominently displayed right close to the exit.*

Keeping this experience as a vivid memory, any time I was assigned to a different store, I took great care to walk around and look for high value items that were not securely displayed. I would call the store manager over and advise that the items be relocated to a more secure location within the store. To my disbelief, most managers failed to take my advice – in their eyes, I was merely a store detective. What the heck did I know about visual merchandising?

As a second example: I was working at a store in London Colney; immediately upon entering the store I noticed coats worth £250 prominently displayed near the store entrance.

Without hesitation, I located the store manager and expressed my concern to him. I even joked with him how even the CIA Director at the time, George Tenant, could not possibly protect those coats where they were positioned.

This manager chose to ignore my warning and a few hours later, some of the coats were stolen; just as I had predicted. When I approached the manager again, I figured he would pay more attention to me now that my gloomy prediction came true. Once again, he failed to heed my warning. I finally got his attention but only after 20 of the 25 coats were stolen.

At this same location, there are two big retailers who shared a single toilet facility located outside of both stores. Shoplifters knew this and would steal from one store, head to the direction of the toilet, pass through the other store and escape.

When they were stopped and questioned by our store security, they would always mention they were on their way to the toilet. They were correct about heading in that direction; given the location of the toilet.

The mere location of the toilet caused the stores to lose thousands of pounds to shoplifting. Yet neither store's management could pinpoint the location of the toilet as one of the primary causes for their shrinkage.

I share these stories with you to emphasize a very important point: Shoplifting occurs in most retail stores simply because it is allowed to take place.

> *Shoplifting is a crime of opportunity; eliminate the opportunity and you reduce its possibility.*

Figure 23: To increase sales yet fail to reduce profit draining activities is false economy

To increase sales yet fail to reduce profit draining activities is false economy. Many retailers feel loss prevention is something that they could do if they had the resources.

The reality is: it is something that you cannot afford not to do because no retailer can become profitable without implementing effective loss prevention measures.

Senior management's failure to prioritise

Ninety to 95% of retail loss prevention department managers are ex-service personnel. As a result of their law enforcement background, they take the law enforcement approach to their work. They focus mainly on arresting shoplifters and dishonest employees.

While it is true that shoplifting and employee theft accounts for almost 70% of retail shrinkage, they are not the sole cause of shrinkage. Furthermore, shoplifting and employee dishonesty cannot be tackled by solely arresting individuals.

Preventative measures such as good store design and visual merchandise displays; as I mentioned in the case of Harrods, are required to make any preventative measure effective.

Figure 24: Many retail loss prevention managers know very little about store design and visual merchandising

However, due to the fact that there are still retail loss prevention managers who know very little about store design and visual merchandising; many of them are unable to incorporate these aspects into their loss prevention strategies. As a result most loss prevention measures fail.

Outsourcing loss prevention without a mechanism for accountability

> "The average retailer makes a 1% net profit out of each dollar and the average industry shrinkage percentage is 2.6%. This means that shrinkage is almost three times the average retailer's profit margin. By reducing retail shrinkage by 50% – from 2.6 cents to 1.3 cents, a retailer could more than double his profits: from 1 cent to 2.3 cents. (Crosset Company newsletter." June 2010).

Some retailers outsource their loss prevention department to outside contractors. As laudable as this may seem, it is a seriously flawed idea because retailers are sometimes incapable of clearly articulating their expected outcome.

When a job is subcontracted, there is usually an expected outcome. However, if the retailer outsourcing the job cannot articulate their expected outcome, it is difficult to hold the contractor accountable.

Wal-Mart founder Sam Walton once described retail shrinkage as a "profit killer". He was right. High shrinkage is responsible for the death of many retail organisations.

The benefit of a good store design and visual merchandising display is increased sales. So as you develop the plan your store design or visual merchandising display plans, you need to ensure that the safety of the merchandises remain paramount.

In the final analysis you are in business to make profit. And you cannot make profit if you increase sales at the expense of the security of your merchandises.

Without losing the original purpose of your store design and visual merchandising display, you can apply changes to the way in which fixtures are arranged in your store in order to decrease the chances of shoplifting.

One way of doing this is to locate smaller items in places that are visible to employees. Furthermore, positioning employees in key areas of the store is a good strategy to raise the apprehension of shoplifters.

Larger products need to be placed in smaller quantities to prevent the store from appearing cluttered. Poor display of large products can obscure the view of employees and increase the possibility for shoplifting.

Aisles and shelves need to be properly labelled to ensure customers can easily and quickly locate merchandises.

In addition to labelling; installing proper lighting will attract buyers to merchandise as well as allow your employees to observe the surroundings easily.

There is no fool-proof way of preventing shoplifting. However, the installation of security systems such as CCTV and mirrors can reduce incidence of shoplifting in your store. Security mirrors optimize employee's view of the store and reduce blind spots.

How to increase your sales and simultaneously increase your profit?

The following are effective steps for increasing sales and profit with a good store design and merchandising display:

Step 1:
Locate smaller products close to areas that employees frequent to reduce the risk of shoplifting.

Step 2:
Reduce the number of large products on display to allow store employees unhindered views of the store.

Step 3:
Position employees in key areas of the store to increase overall security.

Step 4:
Install security mirrors in the store to reduce blind spots and increase surveillance.

Step 5:

Use CCTV in areas that are not regularly frequented by employees and locate high ticket items under cameras.

Step 6:

Ensure your Loss Prevention Department is involved in the planning of your store design and visual merchandising display.

Years ago, shoplifting was confined to the homeless out for food and drink or drug addicts wishing to feed their habit. Today shoplifting is conducted by retail crime gangs using more sophisticated methods, never before seen in the industry.

Within four minutes, an organised retail crime gang can steal seven thousand pounds worth of products from your store. Think about this the next time you develop your store design and visual merchandising display strategy.

Summary

Since 2007, twenty-four thousand four hundred and forty-six (24, 446) large and medium size retail stores close down resulting in two hundred and nineteen thousand five hundred and two thousand (219,502) retail staff losing their jobs.

These days, one can almost walk around the High Street and take a bet with hundred per cent accuracy on which High Street retailer will be out of business the next week, month or year.

If someone was to place a gun to my head and force me to choose the top five High Street retailers who will cease to exist five years from today, my pick will be the following:

- PC World
- Staples
- WH Smith
- HMV
- Dixons

When they eventually close shop, they will blame the recession and difficult trading conditions.

However, what I have proved in this books is, success or failure in retail has little to do with external factors.

Retailers fail because they do not give thought to the things we have discussed in this book. It is my hope that you immediately put the information you have learnt into action in your business.

I have tried to make the information as practical as possible in order for them to be easily implemented. I have done my part, it is your turn.

Good luck!

Great Books by Romeo

Book Romeo now!
+44(0)78 650 49508
romeo@theprofitexperts.co.uk

27.9% The Most Effective Retail Shrinkage Reduction Technologies

Prior to investing in any technology, there are vital questions that need to answered; those questions along with their answers can be found in this e-book.

This e-book was conceived out of our own desperate efforts to answer those questions.

What you will learn:

- Technologies That Prevent Employee Theft
- Technologies That Prevent Shoplifting

- Receiving Technologies
- Multi-purpose Technologies

12.24% The Most Effective Retail Employee Error Reduction Strategies

Employee errors in pricing, accounting and receiving contribute approximately 18% of retail shrinkage; this equates to £18,623 in losses to an average supermarket or store and almost £49,679 in losses to a superstore. This means that a store or supermarket that operates with a 1% net profit will need to make an additional £3million in annual sales in order to recover profit lost due to employee errors. By the same measure a typical hyper store will need to increase its sales by £8million.

You will learn:

- Constitutes as Retail Employee Error
- to Calculate the Cost of Employee Error
- to Calculate Additional Sales Required to Recover Losses Caused by Employee Error
- of Employee Error
- to Reduce Employee Error
- Ultimate Employee Error Prevention Formula
- to Apply the Lessons from This E-Book to Your Business

43.5% The Most Effective Retail Profit Protection Strategies

The retail landscape is changing rapidly with the constant increase in internet shopping. From 2005 to 2009, the online shopping population grew to 1.6 billion.

It is predicted to rise to 2.3 billion by 2014 with gross revenue totalling $778.6 billion. This is bad news for traditional brick and mortar retail businesses.

The question is: are you prepared? You will find your answer in this eBook.

What you will learn:

- The Conventional Approach to Loss prevention
- Why Loss Prevention is Critical to Retail
- Loss Prevention Spending vs Return on Investment
- What You Are Losing
- Profit vs Sales Calculation
- How to Create a Culture of Loss Prevention
- Effective Shrinkage Management Strategies
- The Ultimate Profit Protection Formula

24.5% The Most Effective Perishable And Non-Perishable Shrinkage Reduction Strategies

This e-book is jam packed with information on the causes of retail shrinkage, types of retail shrinkage, the cost of shrinkage to the retail industry and how shrinkage can be prevented. It is a comprehensive e-book on how and why shrinkage occurs and it provides a step-by-step guide on how to prevent shrinkage.

You will learn:

- An Introduction to Perishable Shrinkage
- Breakdown of Perishable Shrinkage
- Causes of Perishable Shrinkage
- How to Prevent Perishable Shrinkage
- The Ultimate Perishable Shrinkage Prevention Formula
- An Introduction to Non-Perishable Shrinkage
- Classification of Non-Perishable Shrinkage
- Breakdown of Non-Perishable Shrinkage

- Strategies for Preventing Non-Perishable Shrinkage
- The Ultimate Non-Perishable Shrinkage Prevention Formula
- How to Apply The Lessons From This E-Book to Your Business

27.8% The Most Effective Retail Employee Theft Reduction Strategies

The majority of retail employees are decent people who go to work each day to serve their customers and make their living.

However, there are the rotten apples that contaminate the good names of the rest.

This e-book is an instructional guide to retailers to show them how to minimise and prevent employee theft in their stores. Like shoplifting most incidents of employee theft occur because the opportunity exists. When retailers remove the opportunity, they can reduce the possibilities. This e-book will show retailers how to remove the opportunities that allow employee theft in their stores.

You will learn:

- Why Employees Steal
- The Process of Employee Theft
- Signs of Employee Theft
- How to Calculate the Cost of Employee Theft
- How to Prevent Employee Theft
- How Technology Can Help Prevent Employee Theft
- The Ultimate Employee Theft Prevention Formula

84%: The Most Effective Strategies for Increasing Retail Profit

The formula for increasing profit in retail is to increase sales and reduce shrinkage. How can retailers increase sales and reduce shrinkage? The answer is in this book.

You will learn everything you need to know about:

- Creating a Culture of Loss Prevention
- Employee Error
- Employee Theft
- Shoplifting
- Perishable and Non-Perishable Shrinkage
- Receiving Shrinkage
- Technologies that Help to Reduce Retail Shrinkage

Visual Merchandise: How to Create a Beautiful Yet Profitable Display

Merchandise display is the most effective form of advertising for a retail store. The more attractive a display, the higher the possibility of increasing sales. This book will show retailers how to create a display that is so attractive that it would increase their footfall tenfold.

You will learn:

- The psychology behind visual merchandising
- How to use visual merchandising to increase retail sales
- Challenges facing visual merchandisers
- How to burst the price myth with creative merchandise display
- The best merchandise display strategies
- How to maximise display space allocation with creative fixtures
- The pros and cons of using a planogram
- The pros and cons of hiring visual merchandising companies
- Most effective visual merchandise technologies
- How to display merchandise for maximum profit

Store Design Blueprint: How to Design an Attractive But Profitable Store

There are three fundamental principles that underpin a retail store design:

1. Attract customers as they pass by the store
2. Entice them to enter the store
3. Persuade them to buy

The aim of this book is to show retailers how to apply these principles to this store design.

You will learn:

- Store design psychology – what you must know to succeed

- Store design – Image selling
- How to use store design to increase sales
- Store design for increased customer flow
- Choosing your store colour and layout
- The best retail store lighting system
- How to wow customers with creative storefront design
- How to choose the right materials for store design
- Designing store for profit – design security
- Store design technologies

How to Market and Manage A Professional Firm Series: How to make 7 Figure annually as a doctor, dentist, accountant, lawyer, consultant and private security firm owner.

There are four elements essential for the success of any business:

1. Visionary leadership
2. Great people

3. Good system

4. Good marketing system

In the How to Market and Manage A Professional Firm Series, we teach professional entrepreneurs how to effectively utilize these four elements for the development of their businesses.

Many professionals are good technicians. They are good at their professions, however, when it comes to running business they are challenged.

The aim of the 7 Figure Code Books Series is to show professionals how to enhance their technical skills and apply similar levels of structural thinking into building a 7 Figure business.

There is no reason why a doctor or lawyer should not be able to easily make 7 Figure per annum. We show them how to achieve this in the How to Market and Manage A Professional Firm Series.

You will learn:

- How to create an effective business system that runs on auto-pilot
- How to recruit and retain only top talents
- How to develop an effective marketing system
- How to create new market for a product or service
- How the attract new clients and retain existing ones

Book Romeo

Book Romeo now by calling:
+44(0)78 650 49508
Or email: romeo@theprofitexperts.co.uk

www.ingramcontent.com/pod-product-compliance
Lightning Source LLC
Chambersburg PA
CBHW051712170526
45167CB00002B/632